CREATE AND DELIVER A KILLER PRODUCT DEMO

TIPS AND TRICKS TO WOW YOUR CUSTOMERS

Oscar Santolalla

Apress®

Create and Deliver a Killer Product Demo: Tips and Tricks to Wow Your Customers

Oscar Santolalla
Helsinki, Finland

ISBN-13 (pbk): 978-1-4842-3953-7   ISBN-13 (electronic): 978-1-4842-3954-4
https://doi.org/10.1007/978-1-4842-3954-4

Library of Congress Control Number: 2018963727

Managing Director, Apress Media LLC: Welmoed Spahr
Acquisitions Editor: Shiva Ramachandran
Development Editor: Laura Berendson
Coordinating Editor: Rita Fernando

Cover designed by eStudioCalamar

Distributed to the book trade worldwide by Springer Science+Business Media New York, 233 Spring Street, 6th Floor, New York, NY 10013. Phone 1-800-SPRINGER, fax (201) 348-4505, e-mail orders-ny@springer-sbm.com, or visit www.springeronline.com. Apress Media, LLC is a California LLC and the sole member (owner) is Springer Science + Business Media Finance Inc (SSBM Finance Inc). SSBM Finance Inc is a **Delaware** corporation.

For information on translations, please e-mail rights@apress.com, or visit http://www.apress.com/rights-permissions.

Apress titles may be purchased in bulk for academic, corporate, or promotional use. eBook versions and licenses are also available for most titles. For more information, reference our Print and eBook Bulk Sales web page at http://www.apress.com/bulk-sales.

Any source code or other supplementary material referenced by the author in this book is available to readers on GitHub via the book's product page, located at www.apress.com/9781484239537. For more detailed information, please visit http://www.apress.com/source-code.

Printed on acid-free paper

Dedicated to those whose demos make history

Contents

About the Author

Oscar Santolalla is a communication expert whose mission is to help technology companies present better, inspire people, and sell more. With more than a decade in the technology arena, he regularly writes in international blogs and gives talks and workshops worldwide. He works as a sales engineer at Ubisecure and has previously spent years in product management and sales roles in the tech industry. Since 2014, Oscar has been hosting the public speaking podcast Time to Shine, in which he has interviewed more than 100 communication professionals. He lives in Helsinki, Finland.

Acknowledgments

This book would not have come to fruition without the support of all these amazing people.

- My family, especially my mother Lidia and my father Luis.

- Mari, who has been by my side from the inception until the end of this journey.

- All my backers who preordered the book during the Indiegogo crowd-funding campaign.

- My sponsors for the original self-published version of this book, Consensus and Havain.

- Bill Doerrfeld, Nando Miranda, Kenny Ronkainen, and Keith Uber, for their invaluable advice and contributions to the original version of this book.

- All the people I interviewed: Janna Bastow, Garin Hess, Janne Korhonen, Sani Leino, Jonathan Malkin, and Audrey Neveu.

- The Apress team for their support: Laura Berendson, Rita Fernando, and Shiva Ramachandran.

- All of you who during this journey asked me about the book, showed sincere interest in seeing it completed, and encouraged me to keep going.

Thank you.

Introduction

Right now, across all time zones, hundreds of professionals are giving demos to sell their products. The bulk of them are doing it online. Do you think that most of these demos will be a success? They will not. Will they be complete failures? No, they won't be that either. Most of these demos will be just average, and the outcome will be a missed opportunity to sell. The result is that your team will need to give one extra demo, arrange one extra meeting, or send one extra technical document to convince your customer that your product is the best solution for them.

Preparation and the right tactics are the difference between successful demos and failures. Think of Steve Jobs, Elon Musk, or Jim Grubb giving demos. They didn't wait until the day before the event to start preparing for their iconic demos. They set out to meet a standard: Make history.

After analyzing dozens of successful demos that gained the spotlight and hearing demo stories of accomplished experts from leading tech companies, I have created this book for you.

This book brings to you a unique blend of tactical advice for all modern demos, and a thorough review of product demos that made history. Each chapter has actionable advice and stories that will inspire you to become a demo expert.

Chapters 1 through 4 present you with a spectrum of demos you can use to promote your products, and guide you to how effectively structure a demo for the most common situations: product launches, enterprise sales, application programming interface (API) demos, and software-as-a-service (SaaS).

Chapter 5 focuses on how to create a WOW moment for your demo.

Chapter 6 shows you a never-before-seen compilation of product demos that made history, dissected to reveal the key elements that made them successful.

Chapters 7 through 9 will help you once you have crafted a killer demo on paper. It's time to get prepared for everything and avoid common glicthes. It also gives you proven tools to be an effective presenter.

Chapters 10 and 11 present you with a view of the future: What are the trends in technology that you can use to stand out?

This book also contains extra material that can be downloaded from www. apress.com/9781484239537. These are the tools you will need for your daily work.

It's time for you to create and deliver a killer product demo. It's time for you to make history.

Introduction

Before cable TV, if you wanted to watch television, buying a TV receiver was not enough. You also needed to buy an aerial antenna, install it on your roof, and wire the antenna from the roof to the TV inside the house. It was a hassle.

When I was a child I saw the following scene quite a few times: A street seller was demonstrating a small, nifty antenna that would easily attach directly to any TV receiver. With this gadget you could save a lot of money and get rid of the inconvenience of installing a proper TV antenna on your roof. The salesman would prop it on any old TV, and immediately receive an array of channels in stunningly good quality. Why wouldn't you buy it right away?

You might have experienced the allure of a gadget like that before. Why, though, did every passerby devote attention to the antenna salesman? He was doing more than simply describing the product with words—he was physically demonstrating how the product worked in a dramatic and eye-catching fashion. Sound like déjà vu to you?

Today's companies put a great deal of effort into showcasing their products. From the commanding rise of the falcon wing doors on Elon Musk's Tesla X, to Jean-Claude Van Damme's epic leg splits between precision Volvo trucks, incredible demos continue to impress and inspire audiences worldwide.

History of Product Demos in Technology

Product demos have existed for many years, but today they are vital to sales and marketing in nearly all industries, ranging from stain-eradicating detergents to Software-as-a-Service (SaaS) web technologies. This book focuses on how complete products, not just hobbyist inventions, are promoted through the use of stunning product demos. Let us first review some moments in the history of product demos in technology that deserve mention.

The Mother of All Demos

It was December 9, 1968 in San Francisco and Menlo Park. Roughly 1,000 people packed the Brooks Hall to watch Douglas Engelbart's "the Mother of All Demos,"[1] a technical session during the Fall Joint Computer Conference.

This was the very first demo we know of that captivated a tech-savvy audience, making demos a show in its own category. The presentation was a collage of visionary computer technologies such as the mouse, hypertexts, word processing, video conferencing, a collaborative real-time editor, and more, all in 100 minutes. This groundbreaking demo ran with almost no glitches and captivated an audience of other computer pioneers including Alan Kay. Not surprisingly, the Mother of All Demos—as it was later baptized—ended with a standing ovation.

The Evolution of Product Demos

It wasn't until the late 1970s and early 1980s that most of the Engelbart team's inventions finally became products. In the 1980s the computer industry exploded, as did the consumer electronics business, which created a space for sales and marketing folks to develop product demos. We started to see plenty of demos emerge for both hardware and software products.

A Magician in Product Demos

In 1984 a new kid appeared on the product demo scene. It was Steve Jobs showcasing the very first Macintosh computer during an Apple shareholders event. Although it was a short presentation, Jobs stunned audiences with the first computer to speak and introduce itself in a humanoid voice. The demo was followed by a standing ovation. If you watch the video of this event you will see a shy version of the man who 20 years later would shine as a paradigm of public speaking.

After returning as the CEO of Apple, Jobs delivered a long list of extraordinary product demos. This series started with the iMac (1998), continued with the iPod (2001), the iPhone (2007), the MacBook Air (2008), and the iPad (2010). All of them were magnificent examples of how to run an effective and inspiring product demo.

---

[1]https://www.youtube.com/watch?v=yJDv-zdhzMY

The Recent Years

What has happened since Steve Jobs? A remarkable example of another executive who presented products with passion was Intel's Mooly Eden. An animated presenter, Eden was very active in almost every Consumer Electronics Show (CES) until 2014. In particular, during CES 2014 he introduced Intel RealSense immersive reality technology. Using 3D cameras and facial recognition, in his demo a girl browsed Google Earth by raising her hands and moving her head to look in all directions, as if in real life.

Tesla Motors CEO Elon Musk began presenting outstanding demos in 2013. Musk's demos are known for clear messages, creativity, fine attention to details, and impressive staging. In June 2013 he presented a refueling contest between two cars: Tesla Model S vs. Audi A8. In less than four minutes, a machine automatically swapped the batteries of two Tesla S cars, while a gas station in Los Angeles needed a slightly longer time to refuel only one Audi A8. In April 2015 Musk launched Tesla Powerwall in one of the best ever keynotes witnessed in the technology arena. In September 2015 he showcased the Tesla X car, an SUV that impressed with its falcon wing doors.

Another excellent product demo occurred in June 2015 during the Electronic Entertainment Expo (E3) 2015 in Los Angeles. Microsoft and Mojang presented the first demo of the game Minecraft for a new platform: Microsoft HoloLens. Event attendees and online viewers were ecstatic, expressing immediate desires to buy and play the game on this innovative platform.

Now the Time Is Yours

Today, nearly five decades after Engelbart, with all the amazing technology at our disposal and the staggering number of products launched every day, we still see how elusive it is to craft an outstanding demo. You can see this by searching YouTube for product demos; the vast majority are boring, uninspiring, hard to understand, or just a complete failure.

This book is a combination of my own experience with product demos, the analysis of dozens of famous and successful product demos, and interviews with experts from all over the world who represent various types of software and technology companies. I have written this book to give you the strategies to create and deliver killer product demos that make a big impact. I want to ignite your creativity so that you, like keynote leaders before you, will be known for your killer product demos.

In this book you will find the types of product demos used today, the structure of a successful demo, the preparation process, tips on what to avoid, and more. You will soon know the answers to questions like these: Should I write a step-by-step script for action and dialogue? What is the correct text-to-graphic ratio for slides? How does a speaker build suspense? Do I need any fancy tools?

Welcome to this journey.

Killer Product Demos

"The mediocre teacher tells. The good teacher explains. The superior teacher demonstrates. The great teacher inspires."

—William Arthur Ward, writer and educator

You might be asking yourself these questions: Why a book about product demos? Why should I spend all this time rehearsing a product demo? Some people believe "I know my product very well. Therefore I can demo it successfully in any situation."

Wrong. I've been there, too, relying on mere intuition to create demos on the fly. However, the results are inconsistent and unpredictable. Would you leave the fate of your business to unpredictability?

Also, after researching the demos that have inspired me over the years, I've found that all successful demos were the result of a lot of preparation, proving that the time you spend preparing for your demo will multiply your chances of success.

Of course, I'm not the only one who strongly believes in the importance of a well-crafted product demo for technical products or services. In his book *The Art of the Start 2.0*, Guy Kawasaki, the legendary Chief Evangelist at Apple during the original Macintosh era (1983–1986) and currently Chief

© Oscar Santolalla 2019
O. Santolalla, *Create and Deliver a Killer Product Demo*,
https://doi.org/10.1007/978-1-4842-3954-4_2

Evangelist at Canva, wrote a minichapter titled "How to Be a Demo God" that stressed how too many startup executives neglect the importance of serious preparation for their product demos.

A Demo Brings a Product to Life

A product demo is not only a promotional validation of what a product does; it brings a product to life. Delivering a product demo thus means going beyond words and presentation slides to prove a real-life value. This is one of the best opportunities a company could ever have to illustrate a product in a way that inspires action.

Types of Product Demos

There are dozens of situations in which you can present a demo. In this chapter I describe the distinctive elements for a few main demo types, grouping various product demos into two broad categories: public demos and private demos. In Chapter 3, I detail the structures of these common scenarios.

Public Demos

Public demos occur in front of a large audience. Rather than targeting a single customer, this type of demo is geared toward "everybody" (general public, media, users, fans). This public speaking act could be for launching a new product, introducing a feature upgrade, or announcing a big milestone. In most cases, this is the time to impress and own the show.

Product Launch

The most impressive and famous demos fall into this category. Product launches occur at conferences, big industry events, or sometimes especially arranged launch events. Because they are in the public eye, product launch demos are a real show that millions might watch.

Example: *Jeff Bezos introduces and demos the Kindle Paperwhite (September 2012).*[1]

---

[1]https://youtu.be/1tvvybPV_LQ

Startup Pitch

In startup pitches, teams have just a few minutes to tell a convincing story about their new business; the goal is to convince investors to fund the business idea. In startup pitches, a demo is optional and actually doesn't happen very often. Due to time constraints, the demo will be extremely short: Half a minute could even be too long.

Example: *"Demo Day" event,[2] organized twice a year by Y Combinator.*

API Demos

During hackathons, developer conferences, and other API-oriented events, many of the companies take to the stage to demo their application programming interface (API) functionality. In these demos, the API evangelist or developer advocate will demonstrate his or her live coding mastery to present the coolest features of the API. Because one of the main goals of an API demo is to showcase how easy it is to use the API, the audience must be convinced that onboarding is easy even with just a few lines of code.

Example: *SendGrid[3] and Twilio[4] have been presenting great API demos in several conferences and hackathons in recent years.*

Video-Recorded Demo

Search "product demo" on YouTube and most of the results will be video-recorded demos. These demos were never part of a public event or sales meeting, but were made as a promotional or instructional video. Once the demo is recorded, it is edited in postproduction and later published online for the world to see. To produce a demo like this, the presenter must be well trained at interacting in front of a camera.

Example: *Thousands of companies produce video demos, especially SaaS products like HubSpot[5] or Podio.[6]*

Private Demos

Private demos are presented to a small group of people, and often involve more interaction with the audience. The most typical cases involve visiting a customer in person, presenting for a client online, or showcasing a product to

---

[2]https://www.ycombinator.com/demoday/
[3]https://youtu.be/jwQ9rfz07vO
[4]https://youtu.be/0pxSfjtn5XY
[5]https://youtu.be/mTThPFOi5RE
[6]https://youtu.be/GLV3djU_UDs

internal company stakeholders. These demos are usually longer and provide time for specific details. Depending on the setting, the presenter might be standing or sitting; his or her challenge will be to connect to a group of people with diverse backgrounds.

Presales Meeting

This is presumably the most common type of product demo. At particular stages in the sales process, a sales engineer (or someone with an equivalent technical and customer-facing role) will present a number of product capabilities and ignite a conversation on business use cases. The goal is to convince potential clients that the product is a suitable solution to the company's problems and thus move them along in the sales process.

Example: *Thousands of enterprise software companies such as Red Hat[7] and SAP.[8]*

Trade Show Demo

If your company has rented a demo booth at a trade show, you will have the opportunity to present product demos to anyone that walks by. You must have an impressive overview demo prepared for the curious passerby. Sometimes, a qualified prospect will be present and this will be your long-awaited opportunity for a demo. Due to the boisterous atmosphere of trade shows, demos for business-to-consumer (B2C) products are easier to arrange. Why? Because you can easily prove value to an end consumer with just one or two key capabilities. A mobile app that splits payments with friends, for example, is simple to demonstrate and communicate end user value. On the other hand, a business-to-business (B2B) software solution, such as an enterprise resource management system with dozens of modules, will take more effort to demo effectively. Thus, it's good practice for B2B teams to prepare two demos for trade shows: a short overview demo intended for new and unqualified prospects and a more in-depth technical demo intended for decision makers or prospects more advanced in the sales funnel.

Example: *Demo booths at CES[9] (Las Vegas), Mobile World Congress[10] (Barcelona), and similar events.*

---

[7]https://www.redhat.com/en
[8]https://www.sap.com
[9]https://www.ces.tech/
[10]https://www.mobileworldcongress.com/

SaaS Demo

The SaaS demo has become increasingly important with the growth of SaaS products and services. They most often occur when a party who has signed up online needs a little more convincing. A stunning product demo can make the difference and convert potential clients into paying customers. As your customer could be located anywhere in the world, SaaS demos are often done remotely with the help of a videoconferencing tool such as GoToMeeting.

Examples: *Sites from SaaS products such as Infusionsoft,*[11] *Optimizely,*[12] *and thousands more.*

Game Pitching Demo

Game developers also present demos, especially when they need to pitch the game to a publisher. It's very common in game conferences to organize pitching competitions in which independent game developers sit around a table and show off their coolest game dynamics to a jury.

Example: *"The Very Big Indie Pitch"*[13] *competition, organized at every PocketGamer Connects conference (currently held yearly in Bangalore, Helsinki, London, San Francisco, and Vancouver).*

Other Situations Where You Need a Demo

Sometimes you need to deliver a demo that is not exactly a product demo. Instead of promoting a product or solution, these demonstrate that something works or showcase an operational process. Some examples follow.

Scrum Sprint Review

In the Agile scrum methodology of software development, Sprint Review meetings are designed for teams to present project results at the end of an iteration. The demo focuses on minute product features that the team has completed. You can do this—and probably will have to—sitting down. The internal project review demo also applies to other software development methodologies, not only scrum.

---

[11]https://www.infusionsoft.com/
[12]https://www.optimizely.com/
[13]https://www.pgconnects.com/helsinki/the-very-big-indie-pitch/

Noncommercial Demo Sessions

If you are giving a lecture or public talk, having a demo is a great complement as it brings action and concrete examples beyond words. A remarkable example of this is the series of demos Mikko Hyppönen showed during his talk "Fighting Viruses, Defending the Net"[14] at TEDGlobal 2011. During this TED talk, Hyppönen ran malware on his computer to illustrate real stories of cybercriminals and other threats on the Internet.

Even though these types of demos are not commercial and often don't involve a product, this book will give you great ideas and tactics on how you can perfect them as well.

In this chapter you have seen how wide the spectrum of product demos is. You might find ideas for new ways to promote your product with demos. In Chapter 4 we will see in detail the difference among them and how to structure each type of demo.

Key Takeaways

- Product demos can be divided into public demos and private demos.

- Public demos are usually one-time events and you are in front of a big audience, as in a product launch.

- Private demos are recurring events in front of a small group of people, as in a sales meeting.

- At any time, come back to this chapter to explore new ways to demo your product.

---

[14]https://www.ted.com/talks/mikko_hypponen_fighting_viruses_defending_the_net

How to Craft Your Demo

"A speech is like a symphony. It may have three movements but must have one dominant melody."

—Winston Churchill, British Prime Minister during World War II

You have probably watched a trove of product demos, both live and online, and both good and bad. How many of them do you actually remember? Forget the funny failures. From how many of them do you clearly remember something great about the product? Why are few product demos remembered and the majority forgotten?

There is no magic or mystery. It takes a lot of effort to create great product demos.

Successful product demos have a clear structure. This structure helps them connect both emotionally and logically with potential customers. The exact pacing will depend on many aspects such as the available time, type of product, and type of event, but there is a distinct three-part armature that the best demos use to their advantage: pre-demo, demo and wrap-up. We will explore this structure in detail throughout this chapter.

© Oscar Santolalla 2019
O. Santolalla, *Create and Deliver a Killer Product Demo*,
https://doi.org/10.1007/978-1-4842-3954-4_3

```
DUMMY PRODUCT: VOICETOBLOG
```

I will use the imaginary product Voicetoblog to illustrate the creation of a product demo. Voicetoblog is a web-based service that makes it easy to publish blog articles. Instead of typing an article with a keyboard, you can just talk and record it. Voicetoblog will convert it to a text and publish it.

Before You Start

Before you start putting your hands on the product itself, first consider two pieces of raw material that will become invaluable for your demo. These are your main message and your story.

Your Main Message

What is the ultimate message that you want your audience to remember when they leave the room? This will be your main message, and will guide each step throughout the demo. You should be able to describe your message with a single sentence.

Regardless of whether your demo is short and simple or long and complex, a single core concept needs to be communicated. Write down that message; for instance, "Speak to Voicetoblog and you're one click away from having your blog post published." Although your product might have many other great features, highlighting the very best one will ensure your message resonates and is remembered by the audience.

As Winston Churchill said in the quote at the beginning of this chapter, both a symphony and a speech must have one dominant melody. We can say the same about a product demo; your main message will be the dominant melody.

Your Story

The vast majority of outstanding products have a story behind them. The story can originate from the creators of the product, founders of the company, real users, or even fictitious characters that are part of the product's brand. In the event the main feature doesn't have a story that fits the demo, you must craft one yourself.

Stories are powerful in connecting data and technology with real life, which makes your demo compelling and easier to understand. For instance, a story for Voicetoblog could be, "Through my work with Voicetoblog I have the unique opportunity to help empower the disabled. Take Jerry, a Parkinson's disease sufferer who can't hold a pen to write or a keyboard to type. He uses Voicetoblog to capture his ideas, and his voice has been converted to educational and inspirational articles that touch many lives." Table 3-1 shows the example of Voicetoblog's message and story.

Table 3-1. Voicetoblog's Main Message and Story

Main Message	Story
Tell your message to Voicetoblog and you're one click away from having your blog post published.	Through my work with Voicetoblog I have the unique opportunity to help empower the disabled. Take Jerry, a Parkinson's disease sufferer who can't hold a pen to write or a keyboard to type. He uses Voicetoblog to capture his ideas, and his voice has been converted to educational and inspirational articles that touch many lives.

Does the content of Table 3-1 sound easy to understand? Yes, it does. Writing down your main message and story from the outset is the raw material that will guide the elements of your demo.

Types of Stories Used in Product Demos

You might find it difficult to come up with a story for your demo. You're not alone in this. If you don't know where to start, check Table 3-2. It lists types of stories that are commonly used in product demos, with some examples for each.

Table 3-2. Types of Stories Used in Product Demos

Type of Stories	Explanation
Story is part of the product	As happens in most of games. In Angry Birds, the pigs have stolen the bird eggs. The birds are on a mission to catapult themselves into the pigs' structures to destroy them. This is a story of theft, sacrifice, and parents looking for revenge.
Creator's story	Product inventors have great material with which to craft a story. For example, Dustin Moskovitz and Justin Rosenstein met while working for Facebook. Both faced the same challenge: Smart people were wasting time in e-mail chains. They therefore designed an internal tool for team collaboration and it became widely adopted. They left the company with the mission to create a project management tool available for anybody in the world. That's how Asana[1] was conceived.

(continued)

---

[1] https://asana.com/

Table 3-2. (*continued*)

Type of Stories	Explanation
Real user's story	If you can transform a very special customer testimonial into a compelling story, it is powerful for both your presentations and your demos. Take Lydia Winters's case. At E3[2] 2015, just before demoing Minecraft for Microsoft HoloLens, she told her own story of how the game changed both her own life and the lives of thousands of people around the world.
Allusion to famous fiction story	To promote the Macintosh, Steve Jobs said that "IBM wants to dominate" and become "Big Brother" as in George Orwell's *1984*. Apple is the only hope.

Exercise 1

If you are going to create a demo now, stop and write down your message and story.

Main Message	Story

The Basic Structure of a Product Demo

Once you have your message and your story, feel proud. Now you have solid raw material for creating your demo. We can start!

As we saw in Chapter 2, there is a large variety of product demo types. Each context will require a slightly different structure. However, after my observations and interviews with subject experts, I have constructed a base formula that—with little adaptation—will fit the majority of product demos. It's made up of three main ingredients: the pre-demo, demo, and wrap-up.

---

[2]https://www.e3expo.com/

I first describe this generic structure here, and Chapter 4 explores the makeup of specific common product demo contexts: product launch demos, presales demos, SaaS demos, and API demos.

Figure 3-1 shows a product demo's three main sections: pre-demo, demo, and wrap-up.

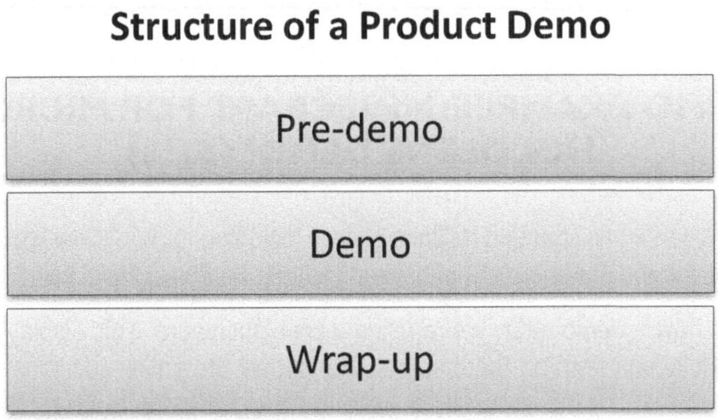

Structure of a Product Demo

Pre-demo
Demo
Wrap-up

Figure 3-1. Structure of a product demo

Section 1: Pre-Demo

A common mistake is starting to demo the product as soon as the presentation begins. The consequence is that your audience will probably not understand or follow you so quickly, and they will miss your opening lines. A pre-demo satisfies two important objectives: It introduces the presenter, and it provides a context for what is to come.

Introduce the Presenter

Write a short introduction of yourself (e.g., name, position, experience) and hand it to the person who will introduce you. At a public demo, it is the event host; during a visit to a customer it might be your colleague. Your introduction should make it clear that you are the most qualified person to present the demo. Needless to say, if you are a "celebrity" like Elon Musk or Jeff Bezos, the host of the event, or the only representative in the sales meeting, you can ignore this step.

Set the Context

Never start a demo without providing context. Don't assume that your audience will understand what you are doing immediately once you start showing the product. Instead, supply a context that answers the question

"Why should I pay attention?" that is likely on your audience's minds. Even if you want to maintain suspense until your best feature is unveiled, give some hints that arouse interest by disclosing precise information so viewers are intrigued to see what comes next.

If the demo is using some unusual technical setup that your audience should be aware of, this is the time to briefly explain it. Last but not least, keep your pre-demo short. You only need two or three sentences: short and sweet.

PRE-DEMO EXAMPLE: MINECRAFT FOR MICROSOFT HOLOLENS DEMO[3] (2015)

[Lydia] "The game has changed millions of lives including mine." "Now we're going to show you a version of Minecraft built specifically for Microsoft HoloLens."

[Saxs] "To show a demo today we're using a special camera. This display technique of putting HoloLens right on the camera itself allows the entire audience to see the hologram."

■ **Observation** Some demos are part of a longer presentation or keynote. For instance, all Steve Jobs's demos were part of keynotes that took around an hour each. In these cases, the pre-demo is longer and usually combined with other elements.

Section 2: The Demo

This is the core and practical section where you show beyond words the value of your product and how awesome it is. At this point, you clearly know your main message and you have a story. There are two main elements you must work on to craft an outstanding demo: a script and a WOW moment.

Write a Step-by-Step Script

I often make the analogy that a product demo is like a theater play, where the actors have everything written during their preparation. Yes, write it step-by-step, or find someone to do it. The order of how things are done really matters. Scripts are more relevant in public demos, but I strongly recommend doing it for every type of demo.

---

[3]https://youtu.be/xgakdcEzVwg

Decide the details of your script in advance. Don't leave a single detail to randomness or improvisation, as that can cause random problems, too.

Six Reasons Why You Should Write a Script

Presenting a sales or product demo sounds easy. If you know the product upside down, understand all its capabilities, and you've always anticipated your prospects' questions successfully before, then you're probably confident that you can demo the product without notes. The truth is that you should take the extra effort to arrange the order of thoughts in a script. There are six strong reasons why you should write a script.

1. *You don't have to rely on your memory:* Once you have demoed your product a good number of times, you will gain mastery and you will rely less on your memory. In spite of this, a written script will help you as a guideline to quickly verify details just before the meeting with your prospect. There will always be some products, prototypes, MVPs, or specific capabilities of your main products that you won't have to demo every week or month. For these situations, having a written demo script will save you a lot of preparation time.

2. *A colleague can quickly learn the demo:* If another team member, colleague, or business partner has to run the demo instead of yourself, a written script will save them a lot of time. This can also add scalability to the organization, in case the sales team is large or customer support representatives also have to present the same demos. You can still be the "demo owner" responsible for maintaining the demo script document and defining what to say; managers actually see this as great intrapreneurship initiative.

3. *Helps flesh out details in advance:* Little details matter. Some sales reps even set up the demo environment to look as close to the real customer user interface as possible. Simple details such as using a plausible name (e.g., "Bill Clark" instead of "Demouser") will make a difference. The next step is to write down these optimal details and parameters on the demo script: the files you will open or upload, the usernames, directories, which web browser to use, target URLs, and so on. Being explicit in a script helps describe details and execute actions correctly.

4. *Identify the ideal sequence of steps:* Yes, often the order of steps really matters. Just changing the order of one step can significantly increase the likelihood of bumping into problems. A good example of this is the first iPhone demo, for which Apple engineers wrote a step-by-step guideline on how Steve Jobs would demo this new product, which was very unstable at the time of the public launch. Even a small diversion from the suggested demo script would have caused a major failure.

5. *Brevity is the soul of wit:* No one likes overly text-ridden slides and bumbling, repetitive statements. Writing a script helps you phrase exactly what you want to say in a succinct manner, so that when you do present, listeners will admire your cadence.

6. *Get the feel of an actor:* Would you like to feel like an actor? Work with a script! For actors, the script is already written and provided—their art is finding the best way to perform it. An actor is not allowed to say anything improvised that is not written in the script. Similarly, a product demo is a theater play, not improvisation.

How to Write a Script

From my own experience, and from reading and hearing about success stories, the way I recommend writing your demo script is in two columns. In the left column you write your lines (what you say) and in the right column is the action (what you do). Similar to stage blocking, the right column includes the details and parameters that you don't speak aloud but are crucial to the performance. The first steps are written at the top and the timeline continues downward. Table 3-3 presents an example script for the Voicetoblog demo.

Table 3-3. Script for Voicetoblog Demo

Lines	Action
To show you how easy Voicetoblog is to use, I'll start by opening my browser and heading to the site at www.mydemosite.com.	
	Open Firefox browser, and type URL. Zoom for easier view.
I'm prompted to log in, so I'll enter DEMO2018 and the password here so I can log in.	
	Type user: DEMO2018
	password: RecAndPublish
	Click Accept.
Now I'm logged in. You can see the username appears at the top right corner.	
On the left bar you can see Posts. From there I find the option Talk and Create New Post and I click it.	
	Click Talk and Create New Post.
Press Record and now I speak for 10 seconds.	
	Press Record and say, "Brevity is the soul of wit" —Shakespeare. Thank you for reading my first post. —Oscar"
	Click Stop.
I click Stop, and my voice has been recorded.	

If you've reached this point and have filled in the product demo script template, rest assured that you belong to an elite group of professionals who are ahead of the masses. Now let's move ahead in the demo script to find a key section that will make a big difference: the WOW moment.

Define a WOW Moment

The WOW moment is the snapshot of your demo that everybody must remember. A WOW moment exposes the best feature of the product and also epitomizes your main message. Do you remember when Steve Jobs literally unveiled the MacBook Air from a manila envelope? That is probably the best example of a WOW moment you can find. Another is Elon Musk's "Oh, the grid is actually zero" moment during the Tesla Powerwall product launch, in which the audience was astonished to find that the entire press conference was battery powered.

Now it's time for you to get creative. You must create something unique that nobody has done before; a new way to showcase the feature. But what is the feature? Start with a list of the best features and capabilities that your product has. Then narrow it down to one to three features you can use to demonstrate something impressive.

When framed in an effective and creative way, great functionality will produce a WOW moment in people's minds. If the demo is for a sales meeting and your prospect is expecting a specific feature that is not in your narrowed-down list, highlight a WOW moment for that feature. Also note that for technically deeper demos, you might need more than one WOW moment.

Ask your colleagues to brainstorm creative use cases. No matter how complex or unsexy you think your product is, with some time stretching your creativity you will craft a great WOW moment.

WOW MOMENT EXAMPLE FOR VOICETOBLOG

Two persons are sitting down, each one in front of a computer. They have the task to create and publish a 1,000-word blog post in the shortest possible time. The first blogger uses a regular web content management system and operates everything with a keyboard and a mouse. The second blogger uses Voicetoblog and commands everything with voice.

Both start at the same time. The first blogger takes 60 minutes to complete the task. With Voicetoblog, the blog article is on the Internet after 20 minutes.

Chapter 5 presents you with additional strategies to craft a WOW moment, and real examples that will serve as inspiration. In terms of the overall three-part demo structure, we have covered the importance of setting context in the pre-demo, and crafting a scripted demo with a WOW moment within the demo itself. Most of the job is done, but this is not the end of the presentation quite yet.

Section 3: Wrap-Up

Another typical mistake in product demos is that once finished, the presenter rushes to say "That was my demo," "This is pretty much all," or "Thank you." If you do so, you are losing a great opportunity to inspire your audience and leave them with a desire to buy.

The best way to wrap up your demo is by doing two things:

1. *Reiterate the message:* Repeat your main message again to make it clear, sticky, and unforgettable. Otherwise the result can be, "Okay, this was impressive but what was the point?"

2. *Call to action:* Your last words must be a call to action, such as explaining when the product is going to be launched; how it can be ordered, preordered, or downloaded; what the price is; and so on. Similar to the pre-demo, keep the wrap-up as short as two or three sentences.

Exercise 2: Your Product Demo Structure

Now that we've covered the full structure of a product demo, with its three main sections and their subsections, it's time for you to take a stab at formulating your own:

Pre-demo	**Introduce the presenter**
	Set the context
Demo	**Script (step by step)**
	WOW moment
Wrap-up	**Reiterate the message**
	Call to action

▓ **Note** You can find a copy of this template in Appendix A, or go to www.apress.com/9781484239537 and click Extra Material to access the Structure of a Product Demo worksheet.

Where Can I Use My Main Message and Story?

In case you don't know where to insert the message and story you wrote earlier in this chapter, Table 3-4 gives you some hints on where to use your main message and story.

Table 3-4. Where to Use Your Main Message and Story

	Main Message	Story
Introduce the presenter	Not here	Tell the story of the inventor
Set the context	You can give some hints of the main message	Mention the story to make this explanation more concrete; story of user
Script	The main message must be clearly shown at some moment	Mention the story in specific moments to make it more concrete or use the story of how the product has improved a user's work in a concrete way
WOW moment	Some WOW moments can fit with the main message or goal	Illustrate and emphasize the story
Reiterate the message	Connect main message with what's just been shown	Connect story with what's just been shown
Call to action	Not here	Not here

As you can see, there are some special sections in the demo where you can use the main message and story. Taking your time to do this can be extremely powerful and beneficial. Chapter 4 will help you to adapt this generic structure to more specific types of demos such as presales, SaaS, and API demos.

Key Takeaways

- Before you start preparing your demo, make sure you have a main message and a story.

- Your demo needs a structure. The recommended structure in this book has three main sections: pre-demo, demo, and wrap-up. Every section has a specific purpose and some subsections.

- You should write a step-by-step script for your demo.

- You should also create a WOW moment, which people will remember the most.

Unique Demo Structures and Timelines

"Use technology to serve, but don't lose the personal touch."

—Patricia Fripp, executive speech coach and
sales presentation skills trainer

In Chapter 3 we learned a basic structure that ensures effective demos that inspire action. However, you might think that your demos don't fully fit into the structure described in this book. Indeed, there is not a one-size-fits-all structure for product demos. For most people, demos occur repeatedly throughout the sales process and their structures change slightly for varying time lengths, audiences, and functional breadth.

© Oscar Santolalla 2019
O. Santolalla, *Create and Deliver a Killer Product Demo*,
https://doi.org/10.1007/978-1-4842-3954-4_4

In this chapter I provide a discussion of four of the most common types of demos, each with its own unique structure:

- Product launch demos.

- Presales demos.

- SaaS demos.

- API demos.

Product Launch Demos

Sometimes the product demo is more than a sales and marketing effort. It is a show in itself, like a soloist in front of an orchestra. If you don't believe it, think of all the people with dreams of attending an upcoming Apple special event and hopes of being present when the next revolutionary product will be unveiled.

Most of the product demos that people can clearly remember were part of product launch events. A few of these product demos truly made history. If you have the unique opportunity of presenting a product launch demo, you can become part of the list of product demos that made history.

Product launches are public events organized as part of a well-planned strategy for launching a new product. The marketing and public relations teams have already done a lot of work to attract interest from users, media, fans, and investors. By the nature of the event, this demo is designed to be done only once and will usually be videorecorded. It might eventually appear on video sites such as YouTube. The presenter is on the stage and in front of a big audience (Figure 4-1).

Figure 4-1. Elon Musk and Steve Jurvetson during Tesla Model X launch (Photo[1] by Steve Jurvetson / CC BY 2.0[2])

In Chapter 9 you will find practical advice on how to present before an audience effectively.

You can follow the core methodology described in Chapter 3 to craft a great product launch demo.

Presales Demos

In the world of enterprise software, demos are everything. Because these demos always happen in private meetings, however, the setup is very different from the one we typically see for consumer products.

The sales process for enterprise software is usually long, ranging from just a few months to a couple of years or even more. The sales engineer—who holds the primary responsibility for presales demos—will usually deliver

---

several demos throughout the sales process for each customer, each demo with its own unique message and call to action.

I explain the two main types of demos involved: the overview demo and the technical proof demo (Figure 4-2).

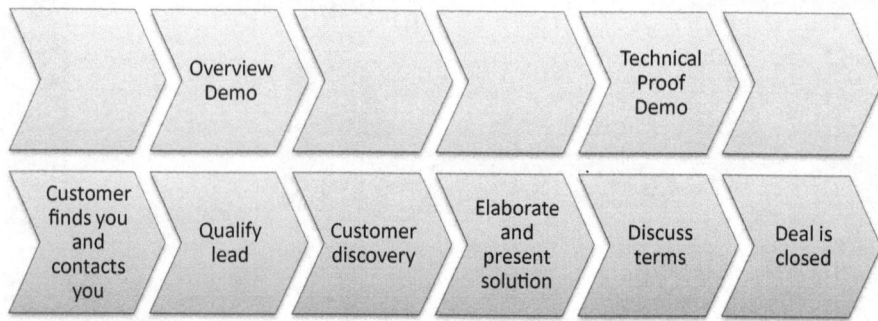

Figure 4-2. Timeline of demos in presales world

Overview Demo

Also known as a vision generation demo, this is a short demo (5–10 minutes long) that you deliver very early in the sales process. At this stage, there is very little customer discovery or no discovery at all. The prospect has said to you, "Show me the product," even if you haven't qualified it yet as a lead. In this case, you do your best to predict the customers' needs to prepare what to show in the demo. A good practice is to create two or three variations of the same demo with a slightly different focus, depending on to whom you will present (C-suite executive, technical expert, end user, etc.).

An overview demo is a great opportunity to ask questions in the middle of the demonstration: Show a bit and ask a question, and then again show a bit and ask a question until the end.

Technical Proof Demo

This is a longer demo (1–2 hours) that you deliver toward the end of the sales process when the lead has already been qualified, many conversations have already taken place, and you know the customers' needs very well. The sales rep has also worked toward promoting the value and general benefits of your product as a solution. Now the customer has agreed to see a technical proof demo. Your team knows well what main capabilities or modules the customer wants to see.

Often for complex enterprise solutions, you must first create a proof of concept. Janne Korhonen, author and sales engineer, told me that he had repeatedly faced the following dilemma when working as a solutions architect at Red Hat Finland: "How do I demo Linux?" How do you demo something that has a huge number of components and as a whole is perceived as abstract? The answer has been the creation of specific use cases or a proof of concept, usually with the help of technical people from the customer's side.

In technical proof demos, the number and diversity of people attending the demo can be very wide, and this is going to affect how you create and customize the demo. In the same meeting you can be in front of a C-suite executive, managers, experts, and end users, all of them interested in completely different modules. A common mistake is to show too much and overwhelm the customer to the point that the product looks too complicated.

To better understand the difference between overview demos and technical proof demos, Table 4-1 provides a useful comparison.

Table 4-1. Overview Demo vs. Technical Proof Demo (Presales)

	Overview Demo	**Technical Proof Demo**
Goals	Give the customer an overview of your solution. Discover more about the customer.	Prove that the solution that has been discussed fully solves the customer's needs. Convince the decision maker to buy your product.
Your knowledge of the customer	Little knowledge. Often the lead is not qualified yet.	Strong knowledge. The demo has been agreed after several meetings and exchange of information, and you have already elaborated a solution.
Length of the demo	5–10 minutes.	1–2 hours.
Audience	Small, typically 1 or 2 persons.	Average 3 to 10 persons, with different interests. Usually there are several persons coming to the demo and each is interested in seeing a different module or capability. The decision maker must be present.

**EXPERT INSIGHT: JONATHAN MALKIN,
LEAD SALES ENGINEER**

Jonathan Malkin's killer product demo secret is this: "Keep it simple, show a complete solution, and make it look easy to use." Stick to being as simple as possible. Even if the customer says, "Show me everything," you don't have to take it literally. Showing everything in an enterprise product would mean that you spend 1 hour explaining each module.

Malkin suggests sticking to minimum clicks, minimum screens: "One click, one screen." The goal of the demo is not to show the process, but the result. The WOW moment comes at the end with the customer's feeling: "Yes, it does everything we need."

SaaS Demos

People who visit the web site of a SaaS product usually want to try the product immediately. SaaS companies give visitors two choices: self-serve (trial) or guided (demo). You will probably see a button labeled Request a Demo or Schedule a Demo (e.g., HubSpot, Magento). A few companies such as Infusionsoft offer even three types of demos: self-guided online, live webinar demo, and of course the 1:1 personalized demo (Figure 4-3).

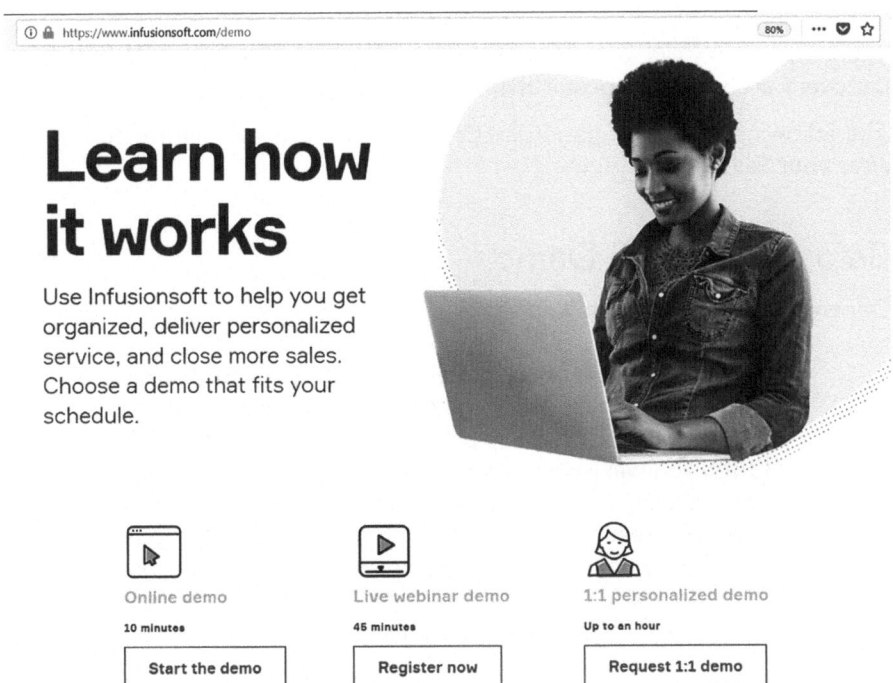

Figure 4-3. Infusionsoft gives visitors three demo options

Unlike traditional enterprise software, in SaaS the sales process is shorter (see Figure 4-4). The demo can be done right after the user's signup. For SaaS demos, a sales rep or a customer service person will walk your customer through the product. Due to its online nature, SaaS demos are remote, using an online meeting tool such as GoToMeeting.

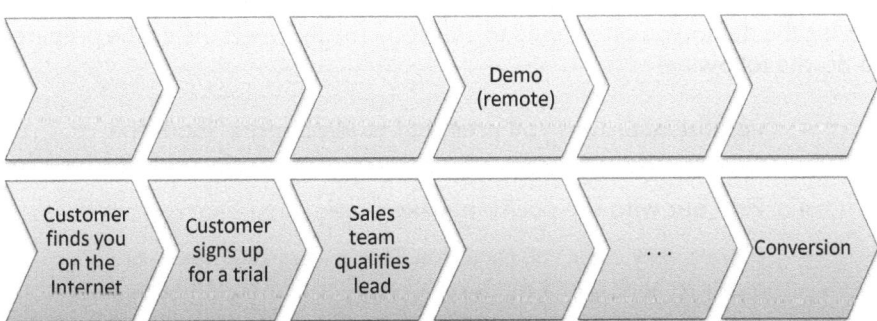

Figure 4-4. Timeline of typical SaaS demos

In SaaS demos, the script is looser and you must adapt it according to the interaction you have with your prospect. A personal touch and customer discovery are more important than following a strict script.

The following is a list of good practices that you can use before, during, and after your SaaS demo.

Before Your SaaS Demo

Depending on your case, follow these guidelines before giving your demo:

- Spend your time offering a demo only to a lead that has already been qualified. The phrase "You don't owe a demo to anybody" is becoming popular and I fully agree with it. Often you will have to persuade a prospect of the benefit of scheduling a demo with you. Whenever you detect that a signup has high potential to become a paying customer, you should be proactive and take the first step. Use your inbound marketing system or any intelligence tool you have at your disposal for this purpose.

- Prepare a list of questions in advance to discover more about the prospect: What is their planned timeline for decision making? What are the main use cases they are interested in? What are their current problems?

- Customize the demo environment with the customer's branding or use cases, if possible. Thus the customer will see himself or herself using your product.

During Your SaaS Demo

During the demo, you often need to adjust on the fly. Nevertheless be prepared to do the following:

- Ask the questions you prepared to learn more about the customer.

- Find out who the decision makers are.

- Have a very clear call to action. This is very different from a call to action in a pitch or a product launch. What you want is to move the customer to the next step in the sales process. Here are some examples: Are you ready to buy? Can we schedule another call with the decision maker?

After Your SaaS Demo

The demo is done, but your job is not over. The following steps will increase the chances of success:

- Write down your observations. If there is a knowledge base, share the most important points for the benefit of your team.

- Send a personalized follow-up e-mail, especially to your high-potential prospects. Don't lose the personal touch.

EXPERT INSIGHT: JANNA BASTOW, COFOUNDER AND CEO OF PRODPAD

For London-based ProdPad, the vast majority of its customers are in the United States and across the globe. As ProdPad product demos are usually remote, the demo time is a unique opportunity to learn more about the customer. This is often called customer discovery. Some of Janna Bastow's best pieces of advice are given here.

- Use the demo time to ask how they do things today, what their problems are, what tools they are using now, how they found you, and so on, and let them give you feedback.

- Talk about them and their problems. Listen to the words they say, listen to the things they ask about, and use this terminology as you talk with them.

- Make sure you leave plenty of time for questions. Make sure that before you move to the next section they got what you explained and you answered their questions.

- Don't be afraid of talking about the future, like showing your roadmap or some mockups you're working on. In the case of ProdPad, the roadmap is part of the product. Also, ProdPad's roadmap is publicly available on its web site. Transparency is something that ProdPad and some other SaaS companies advocate.

As we will see in Chapter 10, when companies have to give a huge number of demos per day, scalability becomes a serious issue. There are some solutions that help to automate demos.

EXPERT INSIGHT: SANI LEINO, CEO, SOCIAL COMPANY, LTD.

Sani Leino was leading sales in Europe for a technology company based in the United States. Their sales and marketing team used a marketing automation system, in which, if certain indicators are met, the sales reps received a special notification. Once, Leino noticed that an executive from a major global beverages company created a free account and started playing around with the product. The lead scoring system gave a notification that this potential candidate would be worthy of a special outreach instead of a normal e-mail message. Leino immediately sent a personalized e-mail thanking the executive for having joined, offering help and tips, and suggesting a 15-minute online demo. He made sure to indicate in many ways that this was a personal message, not sent by a marketing tool.

The executive replied and was happy to have a demo. To make sure that the right people from different roles would be present for the demo, Leino asked if there was anyone else in the organization interested in the demo. In the end, four executives from different countries joined the online screen-share demo.

Leino prepared a customized unique demo, using some generic examples and guidelines and a personalized example specially made for this customer. After some small talk in the beginning, he showed potential use cases in their field of business and with their online content in mind, specially customized with the brand at hand. The executives were very happy and impressed. Leino sent a follow-up e-mail with more relevant examples with the information gathered from the call. A week later the potential customer reached out and bought a license for all four countries. In summary, the keys to success were a personal approach, a personalized and unique demo, and a world-class follow-up.

API Demos

This is the age of APIs. No matter what type of software you work with, you will likely have to deal with APIs on some level.

As in product launches, the presenter is on the stage and in front of a big or midsize audience. Many of the people seeing your demo session are there because it is part of a hackathon or a developer conference. On most occasions, they don't know about your company or product and are not particularly interested in you. This is why you must persuade from the start. Use your own words to convince your audience that we all share the same values of the API. If you do it, you will have created a connection between your company and your audience: We have the same struggles and we all are developers creating amazing software and applications to solve people's problems.

API demos have many similarities with the main demo structure of this book. However, there are three elements that are worth mentioning.

First, your API must look easy. Many aspects can make an API outstanding, such as easy onboarding, usability, scalability, maintainability, security, stability, support, and compatibility with other major solutions. However, even if your API excels in all these areas, some are too abstract for a brief demo. It's very important that the code you are showing looks really easy so that any developer could start coding with your API and in just a few minutes be connected with your service. One of the best examples is the demo that Twilio's John Britton gave at the NY Tech Meetup in August 2010.[3] The simplicity of the code was really impressive. In this demo, Britton created a conference call that anybody could join by ringing a randomly selected local number. This short demo ended by capturing and displaying the full list of phone numbers of the participants (Surprise!).

Second, you must demonstrate live coding mastery. Without any doubt the main element of an API demo is live coding. Live coding mastery involves a number of good practices that, when put together, produce amazing results. Some of these are as follows:

- Make your code short. The live code itself must be very short (less than 5 minutes in total), leaving the rest of the time for the audience to see the results and interact with the outcome. A good way to measure the length is asking yourself this question: Do I need to scroll down?

- Make it easy to display code on the screen. Rehearse in advance to see what the best way to display your code is. This will involve the choice of your code editor, the color of text and background (usually black characters on a white background is the best), and even the fonts. The quality of the projector, screen, and lighting of the room will affect how your audience sees your code.

- Explain what you are writing in sync. Say in a clear way what every line you write is going to do. It will help tremendously if the names of functions are self-explanatory. Needless to say, if you already follow good coding habits, this is easier.

Third, engage in audience interaction. One of the inherent hurdles with API demos is that the presenter is forced to stand behind a lectern. Have you noticed this? In contrast, think of how many times you have seen a TED Talk speaker behind a lectern. Almost never. Audience interaction breaks the

---

[3]https://youtu.be/-VuXIgp9S7o

barrier that is almost inevitable in every API demo. A great example is Audrey Neveu, full-stack developer at Saagie and former developer relations executive at Streamdata.io, who makes a drone fly at the end of each of her demos. With this eye-catching act, she takes the WOW moment off of the computer screen and brings it closer to the audience.

EXPERT INSIGHT: AUDREY NEVEU, FULL-STACK DEVELOPER AT SAAGIE

Audrey Neveu gave her first API demos in 2016 when she joined Streamdata.io, a company that turn APIs into real-time experiences. At first, she did live coding for a mobile application that showed the International Space Station's position in real time.

Presenting Streamdata.io's data visually was easy because the product works with real-time data. Neveu believes that is important for an API demo to have a visual sign, so you animate your results.

In May 2016, Neveu and the Streamdata.io team were preparing for Benzinga Fintech Awards 2016. The company was nominated and they had to give a 5-minute pitch. While talking with the Streamdata.io CEO, Neveu said, "Five minutes is not enough, we need to impact them and make sure they will remember us. It would be fun if the drones can dance." The final idea was using two drones, one on each side of the podium, one rising according to the Bitcoin price and the other according to Apple's share price. The demo ended successfully and gave a great impression. Since that event, Neveu and her drone demos have garnered attention and entertained audiences at several API and Fintech events.

In spite of their charm, drones are unpredictable, too. As the drones are dealing with real-time data, something unexpected always happens and it's usually funny. Demos with drones made Neveu distinctive within the API events sphere.

For future API demos, Neveu plans to build something the audience can interact with such as bots.

Comparison of Product Demo Structures

Now that you are familiar with some of the best practices for these four types of product demos, let's compare them. Table 4-2 shows an overview of the differences in the structures among the four types of product demos described in this chapter.

Table 4-2. Comparison of Product Demo Structures

	Product Launch	Presales	SaaS	API
Pre-demo	Introduce the presenter. Set the context.	Show that a technical expert is giving the demo. Give overview of the solution or proof of concept.	Ask questions. Set the context if product is really complex.	Convince of shared values by telling what problem your API solves for the developers.
Demo	Script. WOW moment.	Script. Customer discovery. A few small WOW moments.	Loose script. Customer discovery. WOW moment.	Live coding well rehearsed. WOW moment is the proof your code connected with the service behind your API.
Wrap-up	Reiterate the message. Call to action.	Reiterate the message. Ask more questions if needed. Call to action.	Ask more questions if needed. Call to action.	Your call to action is this: Try our API.

In this chapter you have seen the unique demo structures for product launch, presales, SaaS, and API demos. An element that deserves special attention is the WOW moment. We will learn much more about it in Chapter 5.

Key Takeaways

- There is not a one-size-fits-all structure for product demos.

- In product launch demos, precision matters because these are one-time events that will likely be videorecorded. Aim to be memorable. These are lifetime opportunities for you and your company.

- In presales, there are two very different tyes of demos: the overview demo and the technical proof demo.

- In SaaS demos, use the demo to learn more about the customer. As you're presenting remotely, remember to never lose the personal touch.

- In API demos, show your live coding mastery and always interact with your audience.

- Use the comparison of product demo structures at the end of this chapter (Table 4-2) to remind yourself what you must pay attention to the most in the specific situation in which you're giving a demo.

Create a WOW Moment

"The most basic way to get someone's attention is this: Break a pattern."

—Chip Heath and Dan Heath, authors of
Made to Stick (Random House, 2007)

During my workshops I always ask my participants to create a WOW moment. First they choose a product, and after a few minutes of group work they must come up with a WOW moment for that product. It's the time to stretch their creative side.

The truth is that a great idea for a WOW moment rarely comes at the first attempt. It really requires troves of creativity, often combined with something else: special technical arrangements, an artistic element, interaction with others, props, and so on.

Let's recap the WOW moment for Voicetoblog. Imagine two persons, each sitting in front of a computer. They start simultaneously to write a 1,000-word blog post. The one using Voicetoblog finishes first using only one third of the time the other person spent.

What you need is a WOW moment that shows the value of your product with clarity, and that sticks in people's minds. How can you create an effective and memorable one?

© Oscar Santolalla 2019
O. Santolalla, *Create and Deliver a Killer Product Demo*,
https://doi.org/10.1007/978-1-4842-3954-4_5

How to Create a WOW Moment

The following five-step formula makes the creation of a WOW moment easier. Follow these five steps to create one or several WOW moments for your product.

1. *Describe your audience.* To assess if one WOW moment idea is good or not, first describe your audience or potential customer in a few lines. Write down who they are (age, lifestyle, decision power), what they like, how much they know about your product or the technologies involved, their current problems or frustrations, and so on. If relevant, specify the stage in the sales process.

2. *List the key capabilities of your product.* For a broad event such as a product launch, the key capabilities can be either the best ones (for a brand new product) or the newest (for an existing product). For a more private type of demo, such as a sales meeting, the key capabilities are defined by knowing the needs of the people you are going to meet.

3. *Pick one capability.* If you have several, that's great. However, you will work on each separately. Choose one specific capability, such as a one-click shopping cart.

4. *Brainstorm unusual ways to show the capability.* Brainstorm—if possible with the help of some colleagues—as many possible ways as you can to show the capability. Think of the different ways your customer can perceive the product's value (visual, auditory, tactile, etc.), how your customers could react, how you can manipulate the space around you, how to integrate the product's story (explained in Chapter 3) in the demo, how you can involve your audience, and as many other angles as you can.

5. *Select the best idea and work on the details.* Once you feel you have a great idea, think of the details that will make the WOW moment polished, impressive, and impactful. Write them down. Details matter.

WOW Moment on Tesla Model X Product Demo

Let's take a look at how the pros have used WOW moments to impress both customers and the media. Table 5-1 shows the five steps for the WOW moment in the "Tesla Model X" demo[1] by Elon Musk in September 2015.

Table 5-1. WOW Moment in Tesla Model X Product Demo

Five Steps	
1. Describe your audience	Tech-savvy, luxury, green-minded
2. List the key capabilities of your product	• Suspension better than Tesla S • Falcon wing doors • Huge touchscreen cockpit • Very silent compared to combustion engine vehicles • Autopilot
3. Pick one capability	Falcon wing doors
4. Brainstorm unusual ways to show the capability	• Car enters into a messy garage full of junk all around • A person suddenly walks very near the car • Open car doors in parking area where the others have parked very close
5. Select idea and work on the details	The selected idea was "Open car doors in parking area where the others have parked very close." Now the details are: • First showed the car with the doors opened. It looked as though the doors took a lot of space around the car. • Car closes its doors. With doors closed two other cars park extremely close. It looks very difficult for a person to open the doors and enter the car. • The falcon wing doors opened by detecting the distance with the other two cars.

---

[1]https://youtu.be/eWIt4Ze7r9Y

Exercise: Create Your Own WOW Moment

The best way to have your WOW moment sooner rather than later is to start writing ideas on a piece of paper. For every demo, fill in the following form until you have a WOW moment you feel proud of.

Five Steps
1. Describe your audience
2. List the key capabilities of your product
3. Pick one capability
4. Brainstorm unusual ways to show the capability
5. Select idea and work on the details

■ **Note** You can find a copy of this template in Appendix B, or go to www.apress.com/9781484239537 and click Extra Material to access the 5 Steps to Create a WOW Moment worksheet.

Types of WOW Moments

If you observe famous product demos and pay attention to their WOW moments, you can distinguish some patterns and key elements that made them effective. For instance, in the Tesla X example, the WOW moment was achieved by solving a difficult problem. For Voicetoblog, the WOW moment was achieved by a comparison.

You can use one of the following patterns to create your own WOW moment. Table 5-2 shows a list of very typical types of WOW moments and their explanation.

Table 5-2. Types of WOW Moments

Type	Description
1. Unexpected	Do something unexpected. Surprise in what, how, and when.
2. Great technical arrangement	Use a new or sophisticated technology that enhances the way the demo is shown.
3. Comparison	Compare the product with a competitor; for instance, compare the effort taken to complete a task.
4. Exaggeration	Exaggerate a product's capability to make it look impressive.

(continued)

Table 5-2. *(continued)*

Type	Description
5. Audience involvement	Make the audience participate in the demo. Make them use the product from their seats and with very little effort.
6. Before and after	Show how things are done today (before) and then contrast this with how things can be done with your solution (after).
7. Solving a difficult problem	Present a very common and difficult problem and show your unique solution.
8. Bring the future to the present	Show something that for everybody's mind is the future, not the present.
9. Something never seen before	Show something that nobody has seen before.

In Table 5-3 you can see a list of famous demos and what type of WOW moment they had.

Table 5-3. Examples of WOW Moments and Their Types

Product Demo WOW Moment	Type of WOW Moment
1. Minecraft on Microsoft HoloLens[2]	Unexpected. After playing for a while, one of the players suddenly created a hologram on an empty table and the game continued from there.
	Great technical arrangement. Connecting the video camera to the HoloLens so the whole auditorium can see the game.
2. Tesla vs. Audi refueling contest[3]	Comparison. Both cars were refueled simultaneously to demonstrate that Tesla was the fastest. A second Tesla started to be refueled.
3. Tesla Powerwall[4]	Bring the future to the present. Toward the end of a keynote explaining why solar energy is the solution for the future, Elon Musk showed that the entire event had been powered by solar batteries.
4. MacBook Air[5]	Exaggeration. The first MacBook Air was put inside a manila envelope to show its amazing thinness.
5. Macintosh[6]	Something never seen before. A computer that speaks and introduces itself.

(continued)

---

[2]https://youtu.be/xgakdcEzVwg
[3]https://youtu.be/6_XEv2f_Uhw
[4]https://youtu.be/NvCIhn7_FXI
[5]https://youtu.be/NGM4PXbUnBc
[6]https://youtu.be/2B-XwPjn9YY

Table 5-3. *(continued)*

Product Demo WOW Moment	Type of WOW Moment
6. John Britton's Twilio API demo[7]	Audience involvement. People in the audience called a phone number and joined a conference call. Later the Twilio API collected all callers' numbers, called them, and sent them a recorded message.
7. The Mother of All Demos[8]	Something never seen before. Douglas Engelbart and his team showed visionary technologies nobody had seen before.
8. Amazon Fire Phone—Firefly[9]	Something never seen before. Using its camera and Firefly tool, Fire Phone could recognize the exact video that had been played on the auditorium's big screen. The video was "The Kingsroad" episode of *Game of Thrones*.
9. iPhone—Cover flow[10]	Something never seen before. The first time people saw iPhone's cover flow.
10. iPhone—Conference call	Something never seen before. The conference call Steve Jobs had with Jonathan Ive and Phil Schiller looked unprecedentedly simple. Audience involvement. Both Ive and Schiller were in the middle of the audience.
11. iPod[11]	Exaggeration. To show how small the iPod was, Steve Jobs put the device in his jeans pocket.
12. Tesla X Launch	Solving a difficult problem. Even though the Tesla X was in the middle of two cars parked very close, its falcon wing doors opened and gave enough space for a person (Elon Musk) to enter and leave the car.
13. Volvo Trucks—The Epic Split featuring Van Damme (Live Test)[12]	Exaggeration. Jean-Claude Van Damme did "the most epic of all splits" between two Volvo trucks that were moving in reverse. This demonstrated the impressive stability of Volvo's dynamic steering.
14. "Game of Drones" by Intel (CES 2015)[13]	Something never seen before. For the first time we saw a drone that skipped hurdles and waited until a gate was open to cross it and reach its final destination.

[7]https://youtu.be/-VuXIgp9S7o
[8]https://youtu.be/yJDv-zdhzMY
[9]https://youtu.be/w95kwXy_MOY
[10]https://youtu.be/9hUIxyE2Ns8
[11]https://youtu.be/bz1ZWvZBGYM
[12]https://youtu.be/M7FIvfx5J10
[13]https://youtu.be/QuXp_mnDH6w

The creators of the most famous product demos have used these patterns—either intentionally or not. This list of product demo types will be very useful for you in the event you need some more ideas. In Chapter 6, we will see a few of these demos in detail, analyzed section by section.

Key Takeaways

- A great idea for a WOW moment rarely comes at the first attempt. You and your team must stretch your creativity until you find it.

- Follow the five-step formula given in this chapter to make the creation of a WOW moment easier.

- WOW moments have some patterns and key elements that make them effective. This chapter describes nine types of WOW moments that you can use to create your own.

Dissection of Amazing Product Demos

"We dissect failure a lot more than we dissect success."

—Matthew McConaughey, actor and film producer

One of the best ways to find ideas and inspiration for your own demos is to watch and analyze great demos. There are many videos of them publicly available on the Internet. I've spent hours looking for the best examples of product demos and analyzing their structures. I encourage you to expose yourself to successful product demos so that you will have a ton of inspiration for your own next demo.

This chapter provides dissections of 10 memorable demos so you will clearly see their structure, main elements, and what made them special.

1. Macintosh launch

2. iPod launch

3. iPhone launch

© Oscar Santolalla 2019
O. Santolalla, *Create and Deliver a Killer Product Demo*,
https://doi.org/10.1007/978-1-4842-3954-4_6

4. Volvo Dynamic Steering video commercial

5. Tesla vs. Audi refueling contest

6. Game of Drones (Intel RealSense and Ascending Technologies)

7. Tesla Powerwall keynote

8. Cisco Live 2015 keynote

9. Minecraft on Microsoft HoloLens

10. Surface Studio launch

Macintosh Launch

Steve Jobs, Apple's Annual Shareholder Event (January 1984)[1]

Length: 3:40 minutes

Story	IBM wants to dominate and become "Big Brother" as written in George Orwell's dystopian novel *1984*. Apple is the only hope.
Pre-Demo	**Introduce the presenter**
	Steve Jobs opens and hosts the event. Interestingly, the product (Macintosh) introduces the presenter (Steve Jobs) at the end of the demo.
	Set the context
	"You've just seen some pictures of Macintosh. Now I'd like to show you Macintosh in person. All of the images you're about to see on the large screen will be generated by what's in that bag." Steve Jobs points to the bag where the Macintosh was.
Demo	**WOW moment**
	Macintosh speaks for itself and jokes about an IBM mainframe by saying, "Never trust a computer you can't lift." At the end, Macintosh introduces Steve Jobs.
Wrap-Up	**Reiterate the message**
	Macintosh is targeted to knowledge workers and college workers. "Macintosh is for the rest of us" emphasizes that this is a desktop computer focused on end users, not computer experts. He then shows five commercials.
	Call to action
	No call to action. In the Q&A session later both Steve Jobs and John Sculley reveal the ways to order a Macintosh.

---

[1]https://youtu.be/2B-XwPjn9YY

iPod Launch

Steve Jobs, Apple Special Event (October 2001)[2]

Length: Three sections of 4:20, 2:40, and 4:00 minutes

Story	"We love music. But it's very difficult to carry all our favorite songs anywhere we go. Apple's solution brings you 1,000 songs in your pocket."	
Pre-Demo	**Introduce the presenter**	
	No introduction. Steve Jobs opens and hosts the event.	
	Set the context	
	This is the first consumer electronics device by Apple, a digital device with three major breakthroughs: ultra-portable, Apple's legendary ease of use, and Auto-sync.	
	This product launch included three separate demos: iPod, iTunes 2, and Auto-sync.	
Demo	**WOW moment**	
	To show how ultra-portable the product was, Steve Jobs takes an iPod from his jeans pocket. After showing the iPod from all sides, he puts it back in his pocket.	
Wrap-Up	**Reiterate the message**	
	Three major breakthroughs: ultra-portable, Apple's legendary ease of use, and Auto-sync. There's been nothing like this before.	
	Call to action	
	"What are we going to sell it for? 5 GB hard drive, FireWire, 10-hour battery, 1,000 songs in your pocket. $399. Available on November 10th."	

iPhone Launch

Steve Jobs, Macworld 2007 (January 2007)[3]

Length: Three sections of 6:10, 10:00, and 11:00 minutes

---

[2]https://youtu.be/lvOXzcKqIPM
[3]https://youtu.be/9hUIxyE2Ns8

Story	Every once in a while a revolutionary product comes along that changes everything. Apple brings, for the third time in history, a revolutionary product. (Macintosh was the first, and the iPod was the second).
Pre-Demo	**Introduce the presenter** No intro. Steve Jobs opens the event. The demo is part of a long keynote. **Set the context** The iPhone is presented as three revolutionary products in one. "Today Apple is going to reinvent the phone." Then Jobs explains the iPhone's best features. This product launch included three separate demos: iPod with touchscreen, mobile phone, Internet communications device.
Demo	**WOW moments** 1. Cover flow (after turning the phone to landscape mode). 2. Conference call with Jonathan Ive and Phil Schiller. 3. Browsing the maps app, Jobs randomly picks a Starbucks café, fetches its phone number, and immediately makes a prank call, talking with the barista working there.
Wrap-Up	**Reiterate the message** After each of the three separate demos (iPod, Phone, Internet), Jobs did a quick recap of the best features by showing gorgeous screenshots. **Call to action** "For 4 GB we're gonna price it $499 and we're gonna have an 8 GB model for $599." "Now, when's it going to be available? We're gonna be shipping this in June (2007)."

Volvo Dynamic Steering Video Commercial

Jean-Claude Van Damme & Volvo Team, Video commercial (2013)[4]

Length: 1:16 minutes

---

[4]https://youtu.be/M7FIvfx5J10

Story	Martial arts actor Jean-Claude Van Damme was famous for his amazing splits. A split between two trucks moving in reverse, however, was a stunt that nobody had done before. Volvo Dynamic Steering and Van Damme made possible "the most epic of splits."
Pre-Demo	**Introduce the presenter**
	No introduction. The video assumes the viewer knows Van Damme.
	Set the context
	"I've had my ups and downs, my fair share of bumpy roads and heavy winds. That's what made me what I am today.
	Now I stand here before you. What you see is a body crafted to perfection. A pair of legs engineered to defy the laws of physics. And a mindset to master the most epic of splits."
Demo	**WOW moment**
	Van Damme completes the split and the camera makes it more evident that the two trucks are moving in reverse.
Wrap-Up	**Reiterate the message**
	The video shows in letters: "This test was set up to demonstrate the stability and precision of Volvo Dynamic Steering. It was carried out by professionals in a closed-off area."
	Call to action
	No call to action.

Tesla vs. Audi Refueling Contest

Elon Musk, Fast Pack Swap Event (June 2013)[5]

Length: 4:10 minutes

Story	There are many people skeptical about electric cars, and one of the main objections is that refueling is very slow compared to gas cars.
Pre-Demo	**Introduce the presenter**
	No introduction. Elon Musk hosts the event.
	Set the context
	Tesla owners have two choices to "recharge" their car: swap or full recharge. Musk tells the audience that two cars are going to be recharged simultaneously: a Tesla Model S and an Audi A8.

(continued)

[5]https://youtu.be/6_XEv2f_Uhw

Demo	**WOW** moment
	While the Audi car is still being refueled, a second Tesla car comes to be refueled (battery swap).
Wrap-Up	**Reiterate the message**
	"Our goal here, really, was to eliminate the objections that people have. You can actually be more convenient than a gasoline car."
	Call to action
	"Hopefully this convinces people that electric cars are the future."

Game of Drones (Intel RealSense and Ascending Technologies)

Brian Krzanich (Intel), CES 2015 (January 2015)[6]

Length: 2:10 minutes

Story	Intel and Ascending Technologies (AscTec) collaborated to provide drones autonomy, real sight. The real world is filled with all kinds of obstacles, almost like a "giant obstacle course."
Pre-Demo	**Introduce the presenter**
	Intel CEO Brian Krzanich is introduced by CES President Gary Shapiro.
	Set the context
	Thanks to Intel technology, drones manufactured by Ascending Technologies can sense and avoid obstacles. We've programmed our drones to fly the shortest distances through the "obstacle course" built on the CES stage. A representative from AscTec initiates the drone and immediately puts the controller down so the drone flies autonomously toward the obstacle course to find its destination.
Demo	**WOW** moment
	Once the drone has almost reached its destination autonomously, the last doors are opened and the drone passes.
Wrap-Up	**Reiterate the message**
	"The real leap forward that industry has been waiting for is to give drones sight, to increase not only autonomy, but safety. And that's exactly what RealSense Intel processing and these Firefly drones have done."
	Call to action
	No call to action. The keynote continues with a video.

[6]https://youtu.be/QuXp_mnDH6w

Tesla Powerwall Keynote

Elon Musk, Tesla Energy Special Event (April 2015)[7]

Length: 0:55 minutes

Story	Fossil fuels are the main source that generates energy today but causes the CO_2 concentration to continuously grow. This is real. We have to do something. Tesla's solution has two parts: the sun and Tesla Powerwall batteries.
Pre-Demo	**Introduce the presenter**
	No introduction. Elon Musk opens the keynote.
	Set the context
	In the first half of the keynote, Musk presented Tesla Powerwall and its benefits. Toward the end of the keynote, he said, "I think it would be a good time to transition the power of the building to battery-powered."
Demo	**WOW moment**
	The main screen shows the building's power room, in which there are two power meters: grid and battery. A closer zoom shows that the grid meter is at zero.
Wrap-Up	**Reiterate the message**
	This entire night has been powered by batteries. Not only that, but the batteries were charged by the solar panels on the roof of this building.
	Call to action
	The pricing and estimated delivery dates were mentioned earlier in the keynote. Musk closes by saying that we must make this solution happen: "This is something we must do, and we will do."

Cisco Live 2015 Keynote

Cisco's John Chambers, CEO and Chairman, and Jim Grubb, Chief Demonstration Officer, Cisco Live 2015 (June 2015)[8]

Length: 13:00 minutes

---

[7]https://youtu.be/OIgzzAMgnSU
[8]https://youtu.be/Mnmv7yZJyTc

Story	Digital transformation is here. Every business must think differently. Business leaders must take digital transformation seriously right now. This was John Chambers's last keynote as Cisco CEO.
Pre-Demo	**Introduce the presenter**
	John Chambers is introduced at the beginning of the event. In the middle of his keynote, Chambers invites Jim Grubb to join him on the stage.
	Set the context
	[Chambers] "Over the years the one thing I enjoyed so much is taking these concepts and really bringing them home in terms of how a demo really explains what we just said architecturally. How it explains what the past has been and where you find yourselves not today but in the future."
	The demo has three sections: Smart+Connected Cities, Connected Retail, and Connected Health
Demo	**WOW moments**
	1. Using a Citypass mobile app and Cisco services in the background, Grubb does everything needed to get Chambers's Senior Pass. Once Chambers gets the Citypass fully from the mobile phone, the desk clerk says, "Fine. Then what I am supposed to do?"
	2. From a tablet app, Grubb makes a video call to a physician available in the area and shows her a patient's vital signs and real-time video images of an injury.
Wrap-Up	**Reiterate the message**
	After each of the three demos, Grubb showed one slide that summarized the technology behind that use case. Before leaving the stage Grubb showed one more slide and ended by saying, "15 years ago you (Chambers) used this slide to talk about how everything was going to be connected to Internet. And it's happening now, and it's truly changing the way we all work, live, play, and learn."
	Call to action
	The call to action comes not right after the demos, but toward the end of Chambers's keynote. He talks about the change that is coming, and asks "Are you ready?"
	The last slide behind him says, "We are ready. Are you?"

Minecraft on Microsoft HoloLens

Lydia Winters (Mojang) and Saxs Persson (Microsoft), E3 2015 (June 2015)[9]

Length: 6:00 minutes

Story	Minecraft is a game that has inspired millions of people around the world and is present in countless platforms.
Pre-Demo	**Introduce the presenter**
	"Let me introduce Brand Director Mojang, Lydia Winters." Later Winters introduces Saxs Persson.
	Set the context
	[Winters] "This game has changed millions of lives including my own." "We're excited to be able to show a new version of Minecraft built specifically for Microsoft HoloLens."
	[Persson] "To show a demo today we're using a special camera. This display technique of putting HoloLens right on the camera itself allows the entire audience to see the hologram."
Demo	**WOW moment**
	After playing Minecraft on the wall, Persson faces an empty table and says "Create World." Immediately a full hologram of a Minecraft world is created in front of him.
Wrap-Up	**Reiterate the message**
	"From playing Minecraft on your wall to an entire world right on your table, Microsoft HoloLens gives the community a different way to play the worlds they already love."
	Call to action
	"We'll have even more Minecraft news to share in the next weeks."

Surface Studio Launch

Panos Panay (Microsoft), Windows 10 Devices Event (October 2016)[10]

Length: 10 minutes in total

---

[9]https://youtu.be/xgakdcEzVwg
[10]https://youtu.be/_wVt8djoGJU

Story	Some professionals work in studios daily, creating and designing. They use many different tools to get their job done. Microsoft built Surface Studio for creators, for the professionals. It's meant to transform the way they work: "Turn your desk into a Studio."
Pre-Demo	**Introduce the presenter**
	No introduction. Surface Studio is presented as a part of a longer event. Panos Panay appears from the darkness right after a 1:30 promotional video screened on the stage.
	Set the context
	[Panay] "I believe that your ideas can be one of your most valuable assets."
	"It's built to pull you in, to immerse you into the content or the creation."
	"When we say that your ideas are your best work, it's critical that we keep you there."
	This demo had several sections (five presented by Panay), and unveiled three new products working together: Surface Studio, Surface Pen, and Surface Dial. There was a second promotional video (2:00) in the middle of the product presentation. The last demo was held by Madefire CEO Ben Wolstenholme, who drew thumbnails (sketches) for their comics "Mono."
Demo	**WOW moments**
	1. True scale. Panay shows an 8.5 x 11-inch (letter size) printout, which had texts and a photo of Surface Studio. On Surface Studio's screen is Microsoft Word displaying two pages. Then he brings the paper closer to Surface Studio's screen and covers one Word page with the printed paper. "It's a 1 x 1 match." They perfectly fit. "The idea of preview is completely gone."
	2. Using Surface Pen, Panay scratches with yellow a paragraph in Microsoft Word. Quickly the whole paragraph becomes highlighted. Right after that, he scratches with red another paragraph. At first the text looks scratched, and one second later the section completely disappears.
Wrap-Up	**Reiterate the message**
	Panay mentions Mental Canvas and a few companies that are already using Surface Studio. Then a third video is shown (2:00) that includes testimonials from professionals using the product. The video ends with the message, "Turn your desk into a Studio." Panay is back to the stage and says, "It's incredible to see how the Dial brings those products to life. It changes the way you see a product like this."
	Call to action
	"It's a product you can preorder today. If you want to experience it, as I think many people may, get out to any Microsoft store tomorrow and the Surface Studio will be there. Put your hands on and get close to that screen."
	"For $3,000 this is an incredible value. It's for the creators and professionals out there. This is a product that we believe truly brings out the creator in all of us. I think it's going to enable in each of us to achieve more."

Key Takeaways

This chapter has showed you the structures and fine details from product demos that have been made publicly available. As you can see, this selection comprises a wide range of industries: automotive, consumer electronics, games, health care, personal computing, and telecommunications. You can use product demos for every type of product.

Keep watching great examples like these and keep an eye to the new ones. Every once in a while a product demo hits the news and makes history. In Chapter 7 you will see the importance of preparation to ensure a massive success like the 10 examples you just read.

Preparation

"Bleed in practice so that you don't have to die in battle."

—Ancient saying (source unknown)

At this point, your demo is already created, and you have a crafted a WOW moment and other key elements. Congratulations! You're not done yet, though. Your preparation involves attention to a few extra details. Proper preparation will make things go smoother and will also reduce your stress as the presenter.

Plan for the Worst Scenario

I recommend you spend some time thinking of the worst things that can happen for your demo, anticipate them, and be prepared. Take some time and write down the most likely failures.

In June 2012, Steven Sinofsky demoed Microsoft Surface Tablet[1] for the very first time. Everything was going smoothly until he opened Internet Explorer. The app became completely unresponsive, no matter how many times he tried to make it work. A few seconds later, Sinofsky walked just three meters away, picked up a backup tablet, and was ready to continue with his demo.

---

[1]https://youtu.be/4QRWa68MtLc

© Oscar Santolalla 2019

O. Santolalla, *Create and Deliver a Killer Product Demo*,
https://doi.org/10.1007/978-1-4842-3954-4_7

Even though this situation has become popular as a funny failure video, the truth is that he planned well for the worst-case scenario and was ready to take action.

Sometimes, it's very difficult to anticipate problems. In June 2010, Steve Jobs was demoing new features of the iPhone 4 when suddenly the phone could not connect to the Internet.[2] As Sinofsky did, he had backup devices and used them to try to solve this unknown problem. However, this time the issue was outside the devices. For the very first time in this type of conference, the audience had created dozens of WiFi hotspots that resulted in terrible interference, and thus the Internet connection was almost dead. Jobs had to take an unplanned intermission to give Apple engineers time to find the cause of the problem. Once he was back onstage, he said, "There are 570 WiFi base stations in this room," and asked people to shut them down before he completed his demo.

As Jobs and Sinofsky did, aim to have a duplicate device. Also, think of extra cables, extra demo user accounts, a second videoconference channel, and so on. Everything that you can have twice, bring it to the demo.

Only if you spend a reasonable time preparing yourself will you think of and plan for these potential worst-case scenarios for your specific demo setup.

Do You Need Slides?

Today we're used to showing presentation slides at all times. You might have heard and asked yourself this question: Do you need slides? Presentation slides can help you reinforce some key information that your customers could miss during the demo. However, slides are not a mandatory element, so be aware of their use.

I recommend you use slides either before the demo (setting the context) or after the demo (call to action; e.g., how to order your product), or both before and after. Please avoid showing them in the middle of the demo, though. Slides in the middle of a demo will distract your audience, make your demo less smooth, and potentially add failure points. Table 7-1 summarizes some pros and cons of the use of slides.

---

[2]https://youtu.be/znxQOPFg2mo

Table 7-1. Pros and Cons of Using Presentation Slides in Your Demo

Pros	Cons
• Slides can help you remember your sequence of steps or points (visual cues). • With slides you can show screenshots or pictures of something that is very difficult to reproduce live. • You can show extra material such as diagrams.	• In the case your demo is executed on the same computer or device, you have one more application to switch between. • Slides can distract your audience from the real product you are showing. • Presentation software is an extra potential failure point.

If you recall Mikko Hyppönen's TED Talk "Fighting Viruses, Defending the Net,"[3] he did not use presentation software at all, and the demos and the whole talk were a big success.

Be Prepared for Q&A

What if your demo was flawless, you achieved a WOW moment, but right after the demo you were not able to answer a ridiculously easy but unexpected question from the audience?

Depending on the type of event or meeting the demo is a part of, there could be a question-and-answer session (Q&A). Even if the Q&A has not been planned, be ready to answer questions. Look ahead and make a list of the most likely questions you will face. Then, write down convincing answers.

If your demo is for a sales meeting, there will be questions. Remember that what you really want is that the customer talks more. This is customer discovery, and we covered it in Chapter 4.

Also be ready for questions and objections in the middle of your demo. In a similar private demo, expect that someone will rush you by saying, "Hey, show me the feature. I can't wait!" Don't panic; keep control of the situation. This will not happen in public demos.

Rehearse to Exhaustion

Earlier in this book we talked about the analogy between a product demo and a theater play, and why the script was so important. Something to remember from this is that before a theater performance, actors rehearse a lot.

---

[3]https://www.ted.com/talks/mikko_hypponen_fighting_viruses_defending_the_net

They memorize the script weeks or months in advance, and when the show gets closer they have "blocking rehearsal." By following this routine, theater performances meet their goals: touching people and sometimes earning standing ovations.

Similarly, in the technology business, it's not enough to design a smart demo. You need to rehearse it to exhaustion until it looks natural and effortless. The best example of someone who had this internalized mindset was Steve Jobs, who used to spend days rehearsing every new demo. You must have seen how amazing the final result usually was.

Now, you might be asking yourself this: How much should I rehearse? Two factors matter: how long beforehand and how many times. For a one-time public event, you will most probably be presenting a new product. Therefore, there is no demo script ready to read and practice. You'd rather start preparing the demo at least a couple of months in advance so you can rehearse for at least two weeks. The same holds true if you are preparing for a product demo video. Even if you have the luxury of counting on a teleprompter in front of you, don't rely too much on it. At CES 2014, movie director Michael Bay left the main stage after the teleprompter stopped working.[4] Although unfortunate situations like this can happen to anybody, we often see presenters of big companies reading teleprompters almost word for word.

For recurring demos, such as in enterprise presales, the product has already been released for a while. Some people on the team have already done demos intuitively. In these cases, you must practice every time you have a brand new demo, such as a special use case, proof of concept, when there are important modifications, or for a very special customer. Rehearsing a couple of days would be enough.

A final piece of advice about rehearsing is this: Whenever possible, practice in front of a team member or colleague so you will benefit from their feedback.

Rehearse. Rehearse. Rehearse.

Key Takeaways

- Plan for the worst-case scenario. When you start practicing, you will find potential failure points. Be prepared to anticipate each of them or to solve them if they occur during your demo.

---

[4]https://youtu.be/R4rMy1iA268

- Presentation slides can be useful but don't use them unless you are completely sure you need them. Consider the pros and cons presented in this chapter to make your final decision.

- No matter how the demo has been planned and arranged, be prepared to answer questions from your audience. You know your product very well, so be ready to complement your great demo with thoughtful answers.

- The most successful demos are the result of long hours spent practicing. Start rehearsing early. You will never say you have rehearsed too much.

How to Avoid Common Glitches

"When you do demos, you have to surrender to the demo gods."

—Mikko Hyppönen, Chief Research Officer at F-Secure

You might have seen demos that didn't fail badly but had noticeable problems. Indeed, many things can go wrong in a demo, even if you have created an awesome demo and you are well prepared and rehearsed. There are still a number of things that you'd rather check before the demo day.

First of all, let's take a moment and think of what can go wrong in a demo. The following is only a partial list of things that can go wrong.

1. Internet connection is too slow, unstable, or completely fails.

2. The main device crashes: laptop, tablet, mobile phone, and so on.

3. Someone on your team made changes to your software and you didn't know it.

© Oscar Santolalla 2019

O. Santolalla, *Create and Deliver a Killer Product Demo*,
https://doi.org/10.1007/978-1-4842-3954-4_8

4. An unexpected notification appears on the screen or an alarm rings.

5. You go over time and are cut off by the venue host or customer.

6. The audience is really disengaged.

7. A major distraction occurs (e.g., a fire alarm rings).

8. The dummy data are not ready, clean, or well prepared for the demo.

9. Bugs are evident.

10. Your battery dies or the power system fails.

11. You forget an important accessory or it breaks.

12. Problems with the projector or the presentation software.

You could probably find more glitches to add to this list from your own experience.

Top Recommendations to Avoid Common Glitches

Now that we know the challenges that the demo gods—or bad luck—can put in our way, let's focus on the remedies. The following are my top recommendations to avoid common glitches.

1. Test everything in the actual venue at least once, if possible. Usually when you go to a place you have never been before, many things can be different. A demo that worked impeccably at your office can be a complete failure at an auditorium or at your customer's premises. For instance, the Internet connection could be slower, have protocols blocked, require extra authentication, have signal coverage that you are unfamiliar with, and so on.

2. Minimize the number of steps the demo takes to complete. The exact number of steps will become evident when you write the script. The truth is that almost every single action you do can be executed in different ways. A demo is a set of actions or steps, one after another. The fewer the number of steps, the smaller the risk of running into problems.

3. Have backup devices of everything you can. You will never fully predict which device will fail. Going even further, record the demo in advance to be used as a last resort wherever it makes sense. In that case, the backup is the video of your demo.

4. Assign one person to assist you who can monitor that everything is in order while you present the demo. Ideally, this person will promptly warn you of any problem you haven't noticed. A killer demo is also the product of teamwork.

5. Make a list of known issues in the devices and software. Products are not perfect—not even yours—and often you will use someone else's products, too, like a USB-HDMI adapter or the device's operating system. Known issues might or might not arise during the demo, but it's better to have the solution written down. Print out this list and bring it to your demo.

6. If you go to a foreign country, verify everything that could be different: electricity (AC) plugs, mobile band, mobile data plans, and web services with location-restricted or even blocked content.

7. Disable applications that show notifications, disable alarms, and so on. In recent years, operating systems have more notifications enabled by default and they are often hard to predict. Spend some time to get familiar with them. The same applies to many physical products.

8. Prepare an "escape path" for the demo. If time is out or the product doesn't work, you just have to change the original plan. Instead of ending in the middle, be ready to keep control of the situation, wrap up, and finish on a high note. To do that, write down and prepare a few words that convey the core message of the demo. During the escape path, show a screenshot, or just navigate a few screens of your product. For a hardware product, use your hands to explain what the product can do for your customer.

By following these recommendations, you will have minimized the chances of both big and small problems.

To make this last check easier for you, I have designed a Product Demo Success Checklist, shown in Appendix C. You can also go to www.apress.com/9781484239537 and click Extra Material to access this checklist.

As your presentation skills matter for your success, too, in Chapter 9 you will find tactical advice on how to present technical products effectively.

Key Takeaways

- Often a demo doesn't fail badly, but has noticeable problems that reduce its impact. You can avoid most of those problems.

- Bear in mind that many things can go wrong in a demo: Internet connection failure, a system crash, unexpected notifications, a bug suddenly appearing, a fire alarm ringing at the venue, the wrong dummy data ruining the demo, power outages, forgotten accessories, presentation software failure, and more.

- My top recommendations to avoid common glitches are to test everything in the actual venue at least once, minimize the number of steps the demo takes to be completed, have backup devices of everything you can, assign one person to assist you who can monitor that everything is in order while you present the demo, make a list of known issues in the devices and software, verify everything that could be different whenever you demo in a foreign country, and disable alarms and applications that show notifications.

- Finally, prepare an "escape path" that you can use to finish on a high note in case your demo must end abruptly.

Weapons for Delivering Effective Technical Presentations

"Everything should be made as simple as possible, but not simpler."

—Albert Einstein, Nobel Laurate in Physics, 1921

In October 2016, Microsoft VP of Devices Panos Panay announced the Surface Studio.[1] As you might expect, there was a killer product demo. Panay orchestrated a great presentation in which he showed with passion the vision

[1]https://youtu.be/hFP_7dbBZkw

© Oscar Santolalla 2019
O. Santolalla, *Create and Deliver a Killer Product Demo*,
https://doi.org/10.1007/978-1-4842-3954-4_9

of his new product. "I believe that your ideas can be one of your most valuable assets" was one of the phrases he used to emphasize that Surface Studio was made for creative professionals. Seeing presentations like this is inspiring, entertaining, and refreshing. You might ask yourself why there aren't examples like this more often.

In contrast, failed presentations occur at all times and everywhere. During my workshops, when I ask "What can go wrong in a demo?" some of the answers are not truly demo problems. The participants describe situations in which the presenter struggled to deliver the demo effectively. Some of these potential failures are as follows:

- The audience was not present; everybody was on their phones.

- Someone made an objection during the demo.

- Too much was said about features and nothing about the value.

- The presenter went too long.

- There was a lack of emotional impact.

Most of those situations can be solved if the presenter is knowledgeable about the product, and especially if he or she believes in it. Yes, you have to believe in what you sell.

Going even further, you should be aware that the vast majority of products that are worth a demo have a high component of technology. Even if the demo showcases an "end user" product that looks beautiful outside (I wish all products were like that), you might need to explain some of its inner technicalities. This chapter gives you the weapons you need for delivering effective technical presentations.

Common Mistakes in Technical Presentations

Let's face the typical case, and let's observe: What are the most common mistakes in technical presentations and talks?

- Presenting too much information in a short time.

- The level of detail or complexity is not tailored to the specific audience. The presenter didn't spend time researching the audience.

- Speaking in abstract terms.

- Using terms and acronyms that are too domain-specific and not widely known.

- Showing primarily text and numbers, which is no different from reading an article or a book.

- Inability to create effective data visualizations when graphs, formulas, and equations are really essential.

What Makes Technical Topics Harder to Understand?

Imagine that the new product you have to explain is blue chocolate filled with green raisins. Even though nobody has ever seen it, all the product features are concrete and sound familiar: chocolate, raisins, and the colors blue and green. It's easy to imagine how it looks and what you can do with it.

Presenting a technical product is different. Unlike the previous hypothetical example, the key differentiator of your product is usually not as obvious to your customers or investors as it is to you. You often have a lot of domain-specific terminology, along with more layers of abstraction, making it more complex to explain per se. Both experienced and inexperienced presenters face the same challenge.

The difference between success and failure is determined by how you as the presenter are prepared. You must address technical topics differently.

Elements of Effective Technical Talks and Presentations

The following are five elements that are used in outstanding presentations and talks about technical products and topics.

Simplify Complex Concepts by Using Analogies and Metaphors

You will always be faced with situations in which you will have to explain complex concepts. If the core technology behind your product is hard to understand, you must find ways to simplify it. You have no choice.

Analogies allow us to explain something based on parallels or similarities. When Intel first introduced their dual-core processors, they had to come up with an easy way to explain their benefits. The solution was the analogy of a human brain, so "having a dual-core computer is like having two brains." When Elon Musk presented Tesla Powerwall he used a great analogy to say that his product would make deploying electrical grid infrastructure unnecessary in many places in the world. He said, "Cellphones leapfrogged the landlines and there wasn't a need to put landlines in a lot of countries or in remote locations." Great analogies like these are easy to understand.

Metaphors will help you connect your complex concept with an idea that is already familiar to your audience. For instance, a commonly used metaphor in technology is "the cloud," which refers to the Internet. In December 2014, Mikko Hyppönen gave a talk at TEDxBrussels titled "The Internet Is on Fire."[2] The metaphor of today's Internet "being on fire" is that surveillance is a serious problem and we should take action now.

Always Speak in Concrete Terms, Never in Abstract

We tend to speak in abstract terms very often. This is so widespread that most of us do it unconsciously. Let me illustrate this with some examples. Imagine yourself at a networking event. You ask to a person you just met, "What do you do for a living?" The answer is, "I'm building an API that uses big data and contactless payments to disrupt employee productivity." Even if you are familiar with all the words in this answer, can you really paint a picture in your mind? The reason why this phrasing is so hard to understand is because there is nothing concrete about it; all its terms are abstract: big data, contactless, disrupt, employee, productivity, and so on.

A great example of concreteness is the tool Asana.[3] If you visit its web site, the tagline is "Spend less time on guesswork. And do more great work," and the product is described this way: "Asana helps you coordinate all the work your team does together. So everyone knows what needs to get done, who's responsible for doing it, and when it's due." Many similar tools instead use abstract—and very popular—terms such as collaboration, productivity, and so on.

Another good example is Gusto.[4] Their tagline during 2016 and 2017 was "For HR people who do everything." The product was described as "One intuitive place to manage payroll, benefits, and HR for your business." Can you get an idea of what Gusto does? Yes, that's the power of communicating in concrete terms.

---

[2]https://youtu.be/QKe-aO44R7k
[3]https://asana.com/
[4]https://gusto.com/

Avoid Acronyms and Buzzwords

There are some widely used words that also make our message less easy to understand. The first group of these words are acronyms. These words help us to abbreviate compound terms by using their initial letters. For instance, API stands for application programming interface, and IoT is used for Internet of Things. The problem comes when the real meaning of an acronym is known only by a select group of people and is obscure to the rest of the world. In May 2010, Elon Musk sent an e-mail to all Space X employees with the subject "Acronyms Seriously Suck"[5] in which he banned the overuse of acronyms in the company. This is a great example for other leaders to follow.

The second type of these words is buzzwords. Buzzwords are words or expressions that become very popular for a period of time. Companies use these words and expressions to try to sound impressive. Some very fashionable buzzwords today include customer-centric, digital detox, disruptive, millennial, next generation, seamless, and so on. Because these words often come from the mouths and pens of well-known and successful professionals, we tend to imitate them and adopt them into our vocabulary. Buzzwords are really contagious, so be aware of that. The main problem with buzzwords is that many people repeatedly hear them but don't really understand them, so the message is lost. Besides that, buzzwords wear out. Words that sound trendy and impressive today will sound overused and weak tomorrow.

I advise you to search on the Internet the buzzwords in your own field: education, marketing, media, nonprofit, technology, and so on. You will be surprised with your findings. You can always replace a buzzword with simple words that explain your point better. For instance, instead of saying "Our solar panels are innovative," say, "Our solar panels bring a new way of generating energy with 30% higher efficiency than current solutions." Remember, don't assume that everybody understands what bleeding-edge, disruptive, AI, API, AR, and similar words mean. Use them in moderation within the right context, or better yet, just avoid them.

Use Multisensory Elements

The more senses you activate in people, the better they will remember your message. In presentations, the main targeted sense is hearing, as the biggest proportion of the information is spoken by the presenter. However, has it ever happened to you that the only thing you remembered of a presentation was a short video or a photo? Certainly, the easiest and most widespread way to put multisensory elements into practice is with an audiovisual presentation.

---

[5]Ashlee Vance, *Elon Musk: Tesla, SpaceX, and the Quest for a Fantastic Future* (HarperCollins Publishers, 2015).

Aim to be unique. You can achieve tactile experiences in face-to-face demonstrations when the participants can touch the product. Smell can be activated, too, when the speaker narrates a story that evokes precise smells in the audience.

Product demos often fall into this multisensory category, as they are tangible ways to present products and the visual component is a key element.

Tell Stories

Earlier in this book I mentioned that to create a product demo, a story was one of the very first pieces of raw material you needed. The same principle applies for any presentation or pitch. Great stories are memorable, make abstract concepts concrete, and help you to connect with your audience.

Jane Chen is the CEO and cofounder of Embrace Innovations.[6] She always starts her talks with a short story of a premature baby so tiny that he could fit between an adult's hands. She shows a photo in which it looks like the baby is resting peacefully, but in fact he is struggling to stay alive because he cannot regulate his own body temperature. She explains that this baby is just one example out of millions of babies every year. With this story, Chen illustrates what Embrace Infant Warmers are: a substitute for a baby incubator used in rural and remote areas of the world. In addition to this opening story, she always tells a few more: her story of how the product started as a project during her MBA studies at Stanford, and inspiring real stories of mothers whose babies were saved by the infant warmers. What if she would instead start her talks with, "Our product is a cost-efficient neonatal incubator based on a pouch of phase-change material to stabilize body temperature for poor and remote areas"? She would lose her audience. Embrace Infant Warmers are a great example of a health technology product humanized with stories.

Ben Wellington is a data scientist who, thanks to the NYC Open Data program that started in 2011, decided to write a blog called "I Quant NY"[7] to share his own findings. His aim was to make an impact and serve as a catalyst for better policy decisions in New York City. Wellington was surprised by the huge popularity that his blog had, and one day he realized that it was his "improv comedy" background that helped him to make his writing a success. He was much more compelling than a typical data science blogger. Today, he describes himself as a "data storyteller." Wellington embodies "storytelling with data," an increasingly popular term that addresses the difficult challenge of how to present data effectively. Data are becoming so important and prevalent in our daily lives that companies are more and more committed to exploiting their benefits.

---

[6]https://www.embraceinnovations.com/
[7]http://iquantny.tumblr.com/

A great quote from Chip and Dan Heath summarizes this whole idea: "Data are just summaries of thousands of stories. Tell a few of those stories to help make the data meaningful." In short, simplify complex concepts by using stories.

There is one last weapon that applies to all types of presentations, and that is often absent in the technology world.

Speak with Passion

Whether you are on a stage in front of hundreds or in a small meeting room in front of one of your customers, always speak with passion. Show that you strongly believe in your product. If you don't sound inspired with your own product, don't expect that your customers will be.

Don't be afraid of trying new things. Technical presentations and talks are already plagued by boredom and complexity, and nobody wins with this: neither the presenters nor the audience. That's the status quo. Now that you have the weapons, it's time for you to drive the change!

Becoming an effective presenter is a skill that will help you at all times, beyond product demonstrations. In Chapter 10 we discuss how the latest trends in technology can enhance your demos even further.

Key Takeaways

- Often your demo isn't successful because it failed, but because the presentation that accompanied it was terrible.

- Technical presentations are difficult per se due to the complexity of the topics and products, and this makes life harder for presenters.

- There are common mistakes in delivering technical presentations. Know them well so you will be better prepared.

- The main weapons for delivering effective technical presentations are simplifying complex topics with analogies and metaphors, speaking in concrete terms, avoiding acronyms and buzzwords, using multisensory elements, telling stories, and speaking with passion.

Trends in Technology

"Spend 5 to 10 percent of your time looking at the future."

—Gerd Leonhard, Futurist

When Douglas Engelbart presented "the Mother of All Demos" in 1968, neither the Internet nor its predecessor ARPANET yet existed. How would he make it possible to show what his colleagues were doing on their computers at Menlo Park while presenting inside an auditorium in San Francisco? It sounded like science fiction. Nothing stopped Engelbart from using the best available technologies to show his team's research work, though. He used dedicated microwave links to share the videos of what his colleagues were doing a few kilometers away and thus demonstrated his remote collaboration tools. This successful event occurred in 1968, long before we heard of videoconferencing.

During the iPhone launch in 2007, Steve Jobs showed on the auditorium's big screen everything he was doing with the very first iPhone. The audience saw exactly what the iPhone's screen was displaying and it felt as though they had the device in their own hands. To accomplish this, Apple engineers designed a circuit board on the iPhone's back that worked through a special cable connecting the phone to the projector. The alternative solution of having a camera in front of the phone would have showed Jobs's fingers and produced a lower quality video.

© Oscar Santolalla 2019
O. Santolalla, *Create and Deliver a Killer Product Demo*,
https://doi.org/10.1007/978-1-4842-3954-4_10

Technology evolves every day and it also brings new trends in how to demonstrate a product. You can use today's available technology to create unprecedented ways to run demos or to make your demos more effective. You might become recognized as an innovator just because you were the first to adopt a new way to run a demo.

The new trends for demos could come in different ways. I describe three of those ways: remote demos, augmented reality, and automated demos.

Remote Demos

Due to the rise of SaaS products, remote demos have become extremely popular. The main new skill you need to master is the use of online meeting tools such as GoToMeeting,[1] Skype for Business,[2] WebEx,[3] or others. In spite of the miracle of sharing a screen from the opposite side of the globe, remote demos have their own risks and disadvantages. I share with you here some of the top things to consider.

- Interact with your audience continuously, especially if you are the one leading the meeting. Constantly ask for cues: Are you following me? Can I move on to the next step?

- Have you ever had the experience of being on a video call with a friend and you had to switch to a voice-only call due to a weak or unstable connection? Similarly, if you show video or heavy graphs the transmission can become slower. Consider making all your screens and slides lower resolution than usual or use optimized images.

- Consider delays in the words you say, even if they are small. Pay special attention to this when you are not just presenting but having a conversation. Take a second to answer and to wait for your customer's answer.

- Show leadership by having an agenda and stick to it even if there are delays, people arrive late, or there are other interruptions. Adapt quickly to any situation. You don't want to waste time and risk that the demo never takes place.

---

[1] https://www.gotomeeting.com/
[2] https://www.skype.com/en/business/
[3] https://www.webex.com/

- If you are going to open a few tabs on the browser during the demo, have them ready so you don't waste time waiting for them to load.

- You can have a second computer logged in to the online meeting in which you see the customer view (how they are seeing you).

Augmented Reality

Augmented reality opens possibilities to interact in new and different ways with the product, such as commanding with voice. Even though augmented reality products look amazing, it is not easy to create an amazing demo.

One of the best and most successful demos based on augmented reality was the Minecraft on Microsoft HoloLens demo[4] that took place during the Electronic Entertainment Expo 2015 conference. The two presenters, Lydia Winters and Saxs Persson, played Minecraft and showed a new way of playing the game, with holograms that could be controlled with tactile gestures and voice commands. By default, the only person who can see the holograms is the one wearing the Microsoft HoloLens glasses. To share that experience with the audience, the demo team put HoloLens right on a camera controlled by a walking videographer. The video of this specially arranged camera was projected on the big screen so everybody could see the hologram.

Demo Automation

Imagine you are the inside sales rep of a highly popular SaaS company doing recurring demos several times per day. In these cases, a substantial slice of your work is repetitive, just giving demos. This is not bad, per se. If the number of leads is small or if the deals are big, you'd rather offer very personalized attention. However, in SaaS, most of the companies are selling to the entire world, which can result in eventually hundreds of sign-ups or requests for a demo per day. Depending on your sales funnel, your company would need to give from 5 to 10 remote demos per day, if not more. How many sales reps would you need? This doesn't sound scalable. Today there are companies such as Consensus[5] (formerly DemoChimp) that are addressing this challenge.

Demo automation consists of showing personalized video demos depending on the interest of each buyer persona, and getting analytics on how every stakeholder interacted with the demo. To do this, you need to prerecord your

---

[4]https://youtu.be/xgakdcEzVwg
[5]https://www.goconsensus.com/

demo and break it up into specific product features. Besides personalization, the other benefit of demo automation is to take advantage of the answers sales reps receive when they take questions in the meetings. Otherwise, most of the data that are collected will be lost. Those aggregated data can considerably help to shorten the sales cycle and to improve the close rate.

EXPERT INSIGHT: GARIN HESS, CEO AND COFOUNDER, CONSENSUS

Before founding Consensus, Garin Hess worked many years at his previous company, a provider of business-to-business e-learning solutions. During this experience, he had to do live demos regularly. One day, Hess gave six demos in a row that were exactly the same, but just slightly personalized for each prospect. It was an exhausting day and he thought, "This is ridiculous, this should be automated."

After talking with other SaaS entrepreneurs, Hess discovered that inefficiencies in demos are symptomatic of a much larger problem called group buying dysfunction. This problem is caused by having multiple people influencing the buying process. In every company there are many stakeholders, influencers, and decision makers, and all of them have a different weight in the decision-making process. The analytics of demo automation are a powerful tool to better understand the group of influencers and to take the right actions.

Catch the Trends

Be open to adopting new technological trends in presentations, audiovisual systems, sales tools, and anything your imagination can think of. Look at the future, catch the trends, and use them for your success.

Key Takeways

- Douglas Engelbart and Steve Jobs, among other pioneers, once used the latest technologies to give demonstrations like none that had ever been given before. You can also take the trends in technology to make your demos unique and more effective.

- Remote demos are very common today, which is why it is paramount for you to be proficient in using video conferencing tools. Know these tools better than anyone else at the office and keep yourself up-to-date with the latest tools.

- Augmented reality gives new and different ways to interact with the product, such as commanding with voice. Consider using it whenever you can.

- If your company run demos in a repetitive fashion, then demo automation is an effort worth trying. This is especially suitable for SaaS demos, but it can be done for almost any type of product.

Demo Your Product, Sell a Dream

You want your product to succeed, your business to flourish, and your ideas to conquer the world. Throughout this book you have heard stories of entrepreneurs, executives, and engineers, and learned that one of their best weapons for success was product demos.

Steve Jobs believed in the importance of product demos like nobody else. It was deeply internalized in him. Jobs knew that building a great product and orchestrating a supply chain that delivers it on schedule was imperative, but not enough. Apple products needed to be announced to the world with an impressive and inspiring product demonstration. Creating the next product demo was always a project that ignited Jobs's passion. Elon Musk, in his own style, holds a similar philosophy today.

If you want to give the most extraordinary and inspiring demos in the world, you need a real transformation, a change of mindset. If you just learn tips and tricks, you will fall short. Creating and being prepared to deliver a killer product demo will require a lot of effort from you and your team, but this effort will pay off. Start this transformation today.

Last but not least, be ready to take risks and try new things. The best demos rarely follow the status quo. Your boss might tell you, "Just wing it." Your inner voice might tell you, "But I'm not Elon Musk." Ignore those voices. Get inspiration from the product demos that made history, put in practice the techniques from this book, and catch the latest trends in technology. You have something great to show to the world.

Now the stage—or the meeting room—is all yours. I wish you success and numerous killer product demos.

Demo your product, sell a dream.

Structure of a Product Demo Template

This demo template will help you prepare for your product demo. Write down the key elements and phrases you will use in your demo. If you'd like a digital copy, you can also download this checklist by going to www.apress.com/9781484239537 and clicking Extra Material.

Product Demo for _____

Pre-demo	Introduce the presenter
	Set the context

Demo	WOW moment

Wrap-up	Reiterate message
	Call-to-action

5 Steps to Create a WOW Moment Template

This template will guide you through the five steps needed to create a WOW moment, as we saw in Chapter 5. If you'd like a digital copy, you can also download this template by going to www.apress.com/9781484239537 and clicking Extra Material.

PRODUCT: _____

© Oscar Santolalla 2019
O. Santolalla, *Create and Deliver a Killer Product Demo*,
https://doi.org/10.1007/978-1-4842-3954-4

1. DESCRIBE YOUR AUDIENCE

2. LIST THE KEY CAPABILITIES OF YOUR
   PRODUCT

3. PICK ONE CAPABILITY

4. BRAINSTORM UNUSUAL WAYS TO SHOW
   CAPABILITY

5. SELECT IDEA AND WORK ON THE   The selected idea was "_ _ _ _ _ _ _ _ _
   DETAILS   _
                                  _ _ _ _ _ _ _ _ _ _ _ _ _ ."
                                  Now the details are:

Product Demo Success Checklist

This checklist will prepare you for your product demo. Check it and fill it in before every demo you present. If you'd like a digital copy, you can also download this checklist by going to www.apress.com/9781484239537 and clicking Extra Material.

KEY ELEMENTS OF YOUR DEMO

☐ What is the main message you want to convey with this particular demo?

PRE-DEMO

☐ **Written introduction.** Build credibility by telling why you are the right person to present the demo.

☐ **One-phrase context.** Explain the context by giving some hints of the coming demo.

DEMO

☐ **Script.** Have you written a step-by-step script?

☐ **WOW moment.** An unforgettable moment in the demo that shows some of your product's best features in an impressive way.

WRAP-UP

☐ **Reiterate the message.** Use one phrase to tell your audience what you have just showed them.

☐ **Call to action.** Tell your audience what you want them to do next (preorder, buy) and how.

© Oscar Santolalla 2019
O. Santolalla, *Create and Deliver a Killer Product Demo*,
https://doi.org/10.1007/978-1-4842-3954-4

PREPARATION

- ☐ Do you know your audience?
- ☐ Slides ready (if you need them)
- ☐ Are you prepared for a Q&A session?
- ☐ Bring your main device (e.g., laptop, tablet, phone)
- ☐ Installed latest stable version of the software

- ☐ Have you rehearsed your demo at least 10 times?
- ☐ You've got good answers to possible objections
- ☐ Prepared all accessories and props
- ☐ Sample data are ready

HOW TO AVOID COMMON GLITCHES

Before You Arrive at the Venue

- ☐ Have backup of all devices
- ☐ Have backup of Internet connection
- ☐ Write down list of known issues
- ☐ Minimize the number of steps in your demo
- ☐ If you travel abroad, check compatibility (AC plugs, web site restrictions, etc.)

When You Arrive

- ☐ Test the whole demo setup at least once, if possible
- ☐ Disable applications that show notifications
- ☐ Turn off your phone, unless you will use it for the demo
- ☐ Disable all alarms

Index

I

A

Acronyms and buzzwords, 71

Analogies, 69–70

Application Programming Interface (API), 7, 32–33, 35

The Art of the Start 2.0, 5

Audience, 38–42

Augmented reality, 76–77

B

Backup devices, 65

Bastow, Janna, 31

Business-to-business (B2B) software, 8

C

Call to action, 21–22

Checklist, 87–88

Chen, Jane, 72

Cisco Live 2015 Keynote, 51–52

Common glitches
  examples of, 63
  how to avoid, 63–66

Consensus, 78

Customer discovery, 26, 30–31, 35

D

Demo automation, 77–78

Demo script, 17–19

Demo structure
  comparison, 34–35
  demo, 11, 14–16, 18–21
  pre-demo, 11, 14–16, 21
  wrap-up, 11, 14–15, 21

Demo template, 83–84

Demo your product, sell a dream, 81–82

Dissections, 45
  Cisco Live 2015 Keynote, 51–52
  Game of Drones (Intel RealSense and Ascending Technologies), 50
  iPhone launch, 47–48
  iPod launch, 47
  Macintosh launch, 46
  Minecraft on Microsoft HoioLens, 53
  Surface Studio launch, 53–54
  Tesla *vs.* Audi refueling contest, 49, 50
  Tesla Powerwall, 51
  Volvo Dynamic Steering, 48–49

E, F

Engelbart, Douglas, 2–3

Escape path, 65

G

Game of Drones (Intel RealSense and Ascending Technologies), 50

H

Hackaton, 7

Hess, Garin, 78

© Oscar Santolalla 2019
O. Santolalla, *Create and Deliver a Killer Product Demo*,
https://doi.org/10.1007/978-1-4842-3954-4